THE JOURNEY TO GOD

May your journey be gracefilled & joyful.

Fr. Antoninus Wall, O.P.

THE JOURNEY TO GOD

Antoninus Wall O.P.

SOLAS *PRESS*

SAN MATEO

1999

Copyright © 1999 Solas Press

All right reserved.

No part of this book may be reproduced, stored in a retrieval system, or transmitted in any form, or by any means, electronic, mechanical, photocopying or otherwise, without prior written permission of the publisher, except by a reviewer who may quote brief passages in a review.

Third Printing

Printed in the United States of America

SOLAS *Press*
P.O. Box 4066
Antioch CA 94531
U.S.A.

Imprimatur: + **William J. Levada,**
Archbishop of San Francisco, May 27,1999.

Library of Congress Cataloging-in -Publication Data

Wall, Antoninus, 1925-
    The journey to God / Antoninus Wall.
       p.   cm.
    Includes bibliographical references.
    ISBN 1-893426-00-9 (hardcover). -- ISBN 1-893426-01-7 (perfect)
    1. Spirituality--Catholic Church. 2. Catholic Church--Doctrines.
I. Title.
BX2350.65.W34   1998
248.4'82--dc21

To my Mother and Father

*But ask the beasts, and they will teach you
the birds of the air, and they will tell you;
and the fish of the sea will declare to you.
Who among all these does not know that the
hand of the Lord has done this;
In his hand is the life of every living thing;
and the breath of all mankind.*
Job 12:7-10

Biblical quotations in this book (with one exception duly noted) are taken from the Revised Standard Version, Catholic Edition. Published by Thomas Nelson & Sons (Canada) Limited.

New Testament abbreviations used:

Matt	Matthew
Acts	Acts of the Apostles
Rom	Romans
1 Cor	1 Corinthians
2 Cor	2 Corinthians
Gal	Galatians
Eph	Ephesians
Phil	Philippians

References to the *Catechism of the Catholic Church* are abbreviated as CCC. Quotations are taken from the English translation for the United States of America copyright © 1994 and published by the Paulist Press Mahwah, New Jersey 07430

Preface

This book is in the mainstream of Catholic tradition. Its Scriptural basis reflects insights into the Gospel Jesus rather than the elusive, subjectivised Historical Jesus. Its theology comes primarily from Thomas Aquinas.

My intent is to offer a clear insight into the meaning of human existence in the context of its loving source and goal. My desire is to illuminate the dynamics of human development in the movement to union with the God, Who is the Alpha and Omega of existence.

I have tried to avoid elements of the mystery of this journey which would distract from the essentials involved. Nevertheless I recognize that the outline given may awaken questions it does not resolve. However, it is more desirable for persons to have such unresolved questions than to be unaware of the significance of their human existence. Questions stir the mind to life and this is part of what the journey to God is about.

In my efforts to illuminate the stages of the soul's journey to God I am particularly appreciative of the assistance of Catherine and Dominic Colvert. Both have provided perceptive insights and the impetus to develop the book. I am also grateful for the critical contributions of many others, particularly Basil Cole, Brendon Colvert, Leo Daly, Brian Mullady, Fabian Parmesano and Philip Valera. The good in the book is due as much to their efforts as to mine. I find it easy to accept responsibility for the defects, after all, it is a short book about a long journey.

A. Wall

Oakland
November 1998

Editors Note

This book is based on a series of talks that explored the meaning of life. Only when our existence is meaningful and purposeful are we are moved to vital activity. Therefore, a goal of the book is to provide affective knowledge. Affective knowledge moves us to action as distinct from speculation which merely adds to our understanding.

However, affectiveness has different wellsprings. The approach taken here is that truth is based on the twin pillars of faith and reason. When Jesus upbraided the Apostles "Oh ye of little faith" he was not encouraging blind action. He was telling them to have courage and to take the steps their experience of him dictated.

Inevitably it has been necessary to make changes to the flow of language when putting the spoken word into written form. However, mindful of the power of the preacher, we have striven to provide an unaffected rendering of the spoken word. Footnotes have been added for those who may want to explore topics further.

CONTENTS

■

Foreword

Every journey is a process made up of various parts. The journeyman's advancement along the way is determined by the milestones whereby he is able to measure his progress. Father Wall shows us that this applies to the spiritual life as well.

Before anyone undertakes a journey he must prepare for it. To set out on our journey to God, the only true goal of our life, we must first look into ourselves and reflect on the truth that He penetrates every nook and cranny of our being. Unfortunately, this truth eludes us in the helter-skelter of our daily lives. God is always present to us, but we are not present to Him. To make ourselves present to Him requires a spiritual journey, a journey of awakening, a journey of love to Love.

Our journey to God, as Father Wall teaches us in this remarkably inspiring book, is a lifelong process. It is determined by three milestones, which Father Wall calls the three stages of awakening: the mirror of nature, the mirror of Christ without, and the mirror of Christ within. The first of these milestone awakenings is a reflection on the glory of nature around us, which is itself but a reflection of God's all-pervasive beauty. This helps to turn us away from our self-centeredness and represents a definite but still inadequate progress.

The second milestone, the mirror of Christ without, gives us the Lord in all the beauty of His personality as our companion on the way. This awakens a more concentrated love. But we have not yet arrived, as we can still fall by the wayside.

The third milestone, the mirror of Christ within, finally achieves our infusion into Christ, so that, in the words of St. Paul, "It is no longer I who live, but Christ who lives within me." To encourage us on this journey Father Wall appeals to a wonderful example of a successful journeyman -- the very human Apostle Peter.

Father Wall is well able to guide us along this journey. As a Dominican steeped in the theology of St. Thomas Aquinas, a veteran teacher of spirituality, an itinerant preacher and counselor of souls, he is well qualified to describe this journey of the soul. He is able to present the most profound truths of faith and of human psychology in a clear, easily understood and delightful way. His final chapters are a description of the bliss that awaits the journeyman when he finally reaches his goal. The description, as Father Wall points out, must fall infinitely short of reality since "no eye has seen nor ear has heard what God has prepared for those who love Him."

Father Gerald A. Buckley, O.P.

San Francisco

November 1998

THE JOURNEY TO GOD

CHAPTER ONE

The Journey

The journey to God, a Christian concept

§

It is not a spatial journey

§

Catholic Faith says God is omnipresent

§

God's presence sustains us in existence

§

THE JOURNEY

All true Christians believe that salvation comes through Jesus Christ. They agree with the good news on bumper stickers everywhere that 'Jesus Saves'. All hold that Jesus Christ came into this world to bring us to a loving union with God whom we will see face to face.

The most common symbol of the dynamic of Christian salvation is that of a 'journey'. The *Catechism of the Catholic Church* says, "God freely willed to create a world 'in a state of journeying.'"[1] Christ comes to guide us as pilgrims on this journey. The journey will end with the loving, face to face, encounter with our heavenly Father.

Christians often understand the journey in spatial terms. It is conceived of as traveling from some place where God is not to another place where indeed he is present. It entails, in a word, a movement from here in space where God is not present, to there in space where he is.

Many fundamentalist Christians tend to think of the journey of salvation in these spatial terms. They tell us that this world is a sinful world where God is not present. According to this understanding Jesus comes into this sinful, Godless world to free us from this place where God is not present to lead us into that other world, heaven, where God dwells.

Catholics also fall into this spatial understanding of the journey to God. Such a spatial understanding explains the fascination of many Catholics with going on pilgrimage to the Holy Land, Lourdes, Fatima and other sacred places.

Behind their fascination is a spatial thinking that locates God more in those places than in home, city, or

3

country. If only I could leave this worldly place, they think, where God shows little or no sign of his presence, and get to this or that holy place, then I would find myself in the presence of God and I would have advanced significantly on my journey of salvation.

Catholics fall into this way of thinking within the very confines of the parish. How many Catholics understand their parish church to be the place in which God truly dwells and where alone he can be found? So they leave their homes -- the profane kitchen, dining room, bedroom and basement where God is not present -- and head for the parish church where he abides and where they enter into his presence. Again the thinking is about a journey in space from where God is not to another place where God is.

What does Catholic faith teach about this way of thinking? Catholic faith teaches that God is fully present everywhere. It teaches that God on his part is as fully present on earth as he is in heaven. It affirms that God is as fully present in our country, our city and our home as he is in the Holy Land, Lourdes, Fatima or any other holy place. This faith holds that God is as fully present in our kitchen, basement, living room, bedroom and garden as he is in our parish church. For that matter he is as fully present in our home as he is present in the basilica of Saint Peter's in Rome. The term for this understanding of the mystery of God is that he is omnipresent. [2]

To say that God *on his part* is fully present to all creatures is to speak of the objective presence of God to all beings. God's objective presence produces diverse effects in different persons. Therefore the subjective experience of God's presence produces differing relations to him. Later we will deal with the subjective changes that progressively awakens persons to the objective presence of God in their lives.

According to Catholic faith we must affirm that God on his part is as fully present to you and me as he is to the greatest saints. Even more, we must hold that God is as fully present to us at this very moment as he is present to the Blessed Virgin Mary. The teaching of Catholic faith about the omnipresence of God may indeed sound strange. It implies that God is as fully present to each of us as he is present to the human nature of the Second Person of the Holy Trinity, the Word made flesh.

The omnipresence of God in no way conflicts with our consciousness in faith that God is radically 'other' than ourselves. He infinitely transcends our human actuality and all created reality. These two aspects of the mystery of the Godhead daily challenge our understanding of him, and qualify our relations with him.

Saint Thomas Aquinas[3] teaches that God is closer to us than we are to ourselves. At the same time he is radically 'other' than us and transcends the entire order of created being. The technical terms for these two aspects of the Godhead are immanence and transcendence. Belief in the omnipresence of God reflects the Divine immanence. It should not conflict with our belief in his divine transcendence.

Saint Paul expresses the mystery of divine immanence when he teaches that, "In him we live and move and have our being."[4] In his view we are like fish swimming in an ocean of divine love. God's love is all around us and within us.

Saint Thomas points out that, were God's love not immediately present to us, we would not exist. He uses Saint Augustine's simple, beautiful example to illustrate our relation to the creative activity of God's love. He teaches that we are like beams of light coming from the illuminating activity of the sun.[5]

Just as these beams of light need the activity of the sun to initiate their existence, so also they depend upon the continuing activity of the sun to sustain their existence.

Remove the sun and the beams of light would instantly cease to exist.

We might substitute a modern flashlight in the place of the sun called upon by Saint Augustine. If you were to go into a dark room and turn on the flashlight, immediately a bright beam would come into existence. That beam would depend upon the activity of the flashlight not only for its initiation, but for its continued existence. You could not turn off the flashlight and withdraw from the room, only to return five minutes later and find the beam still shining brightly. When the flashlight's illuminating activity ceases the beam of light likewise ends instantly. We are like beams of light emanating from the creative activity of divine love.

This love is not only necessary to initiate our existence. It is indispensable to our continued existence in this life and the next. At the instant in which God ceases to be more present to us than we are to ourselves, *we* would immediately cease to exist.

This radical dependence on the presence of God is true not only of ourselves, but it applies to the whole order of creation. That is why Catholics hold that God is as fully present on earth as he is in heaven.

We hold that God is as fully present in our country, our city and our home as he is in the Holy Land, Lourdes, Fatima and other sacred places. We affirm that he is as fully present on his part in our kitchen, bedroom, basement, living room and garden as he is in our parish church. Therefore, we do not have to go anywhere to be in his presence.

If we were to decide to leave by plane on a pilgrimage to the Holy Land, God would be fully present with us in the departure airport. He would be equally present to us as we watched the in-flight movies while soaring above the Atlantic Ocean.

As we arrived in the airport in the Holy Land, he would be as fully present to us at that moment as we would find him in Bethlehem, or in Nazareth, or along the Sea of Galilee, or on Mount Olivet. This is the Catholic belief in the omnipresence of God. You and I do not have to go any place to be in the fullness of his presence.

Imagine that you enter your children's bedrooms on a chilly, wintry Sunday morning to awaken and prepare them to go to Mass. In response to your call they object to getting out of their warm beds. They protest that God is already fully present with them beneath their blankets. They claim he is as fully present to them in their warm beds as he is in their parish church. This is basic, sound Catholic teaching about the omnipresence of God and Saint Thomas would beam at their healthy, theological insight.

If, then, God is already fully present to you and me, as fully present as ever he will be on his part, what do we mean by the 'journey of salvation'? What need have we of Christ to bring us to a divine presence that already exists to us? These are the questions we must clarify.

---

[1] CCC 310

[2] It is, of course, a mystery how God who is one can be everywhere. Yet within our own experience as human beings, who are a mere specks in the physical universe, our intellect exceeds all material things. The universe exists in us through knowledge. Saint Thomas Aquinas says (*Summa Contra Gentiles* Bk. 3a Chap.68) "But God is indivisible as existing altogether outside the genus of continuous quantity…He was from eternity before there was any place. Yet by the immensity of His power He reaches all things that are in place."

[3] Thomas Aquinas lived in the 13th century. He entered the Dominican Order at age 22 in Naples Italy. He died in 1274 and was canonized in 1323. His synthesis of faith and reason, the moral and political sciences and Greek and Christian thought stands as a great achievement of

Scholastic thought. We will refer to him as Saint Thomas in the remainder of this book.

[4] Acts 17:28

[5] *Cf.* Thomas Aquinas *Summa Theologiae* First Part Q 104

CHAPTER TWO

The Presence

God's omnipresence does not remove his
transcendence

§

God's immanence does not mean he is fully
manifest in any creature

§

Creation is a work of divine art

§

God's presence sustains all creatures in
existence

§

Why make pilgrimages to holy places

§

Why visit the parish church

§

THE PRESENCE

Affirming God's omnipresence, as we have done, emphasizes that God is indwelling or immanent in all things. Our day-to-day activities tend to hide this fact from us. In stressing the immanence of God in the created order we expand our vision to the true nature of the world in which we live. However, we are not espousing some form of Catholic pantheism. We must not slip into a New Age form of religious consciousness. New Age religion affirms the divine immanence while denying or placing in jeopardy divine transcendence.[1]

All religions tend to swing from one extreme in which God's immanence is affirmed in a way that threatens his transcendence, to the other extreme wherein the affirmation of God's transcendence threatens the fact of his immanence. The genius of the Catholic faith is evidenced in its success in affirming both aspects of the Godhead. Catholicism affirms immanence and transcendence in a balanced way that does justice to both.

This balancing of immanence and transcendence is always accompanied by tension. Most of the great doctrinal struggles in the Catholic Faith have to do with this specific tension. Indeed this struggle for balance in affirming both the immanence and transcendence of God is at the heart of many of the tensions in the Church to-day.

Consider the problem of the parent standing in her childrens' bedroom door. Two distinctions are needed to deal with the sophisticated Catholic theological wisdom contained in their argument for not leaving their warm beds to go out in the cold and attend Mass. These distinctions are essential to the Catholic understanding of the journey of salvation.

The first distinction is a clear and simple one. It is one thing to say that God is fully present to every creature in heaven and on earth. It is entirely different to say that he manifests his presence fully and equally in every creature. Clearly all creatures reveal the creator differently.

The second distinction also agrees that God, on his part, is fully present. We therefore are in his presence. It points out that this does not mean that we creatures are capable of experiencing his presence. We will discuss later the way in which our capacity to experience God is awakened.

Certainly God is present to the lilies of the field and manifests his presence through them in one way. However, they do not fully exhaust his creative power. They provide only a limited expression or revelation of that power.

God is likewise present to the birds of the air. They also provide a manifestation of his presence and power, but it is quite different from the one offered by the lilies of the field. Again, God reveals his presence and power in the innocence and beauty of little children. While they offer a very different and far more wonderful revelation of God's creative love, they too are only a partial manifestation of the creative potential of his love.

No one creature or collection of creatures can adequately manifest the infinite creative power and love of God. This is why Saint Thomas argues that creation calls for a seemingly infinite variety and diversity of creatures so they might accumulatively provide a more adequate revelation of this divine power and love.[2]

The Catholic understanding is that creation is not motivated by necessity, but by a free choice of God's love to share with us his perfections. Given this, the incredible multiplication and variation of creatures is the logical consequence of God's loving design to overcome the inherent limitations of created beings and provide in their multiplication a fuller revelation of his love.

Should God choose to reveal something of the infinity of his power, then the vastness of the heavens fulfills this intention. We find our minds stunned by the reality of the cosmos. In it this earth is no more than a speck of dust. Light from bodies millions of light years away reaches us humans staring out from this speck. In contemplating this we begin to have a still inadequate notion of what infinity means as applied to God.

Should God wish to manifest something of the mystery of his being, the microcosm accomplishes this. Matter consists of tiny particles and forces that elude the most complex systems of mathematics to render them intelligible to us. From time to time scientists are convinced that they can discover all there is to know about this world, if only they could reduce it to the elements from which it is formed. To their surprise, the more success they enjoy in breaking down matter, the more complex and mysterious reality reveals itself to be. The greater their success the more humble they become before the mystery inherent in the tiniest bits of reality.

With success in physical science the words of Saint Paul begin to make more sense. "Oh, the depth of the riches and wisdom and knowledge of God! How unsearchable are his judgments and how inscrutable his ways! For who has known the mind of the Lord or who has been his counselor."[3]

Saint Thomas describes God's work of creation as a work of divine art.[4] Just as the artist embodies his creative genius in his artistic efforts and they reveal something of that genius to us, so also God embodies his wisdom, love and power in each and every creature. All creatures provide reflections of their divine origin.

13

Michelangelo reveals different aspects of his genius in his Sistine Chapel, Pieta, Moses and David.[5] Each of these reflects inadequately only part of his creativity. Similarly God reveals different facets of his creative power in the lilies of the field, the birds of the air, the vastness of space, the incomprehensibility of matter and the miracle of children. Each of these provides partial reflections of his limitless power.

To appreciate something of the genius of a Michelangelo one must gather in one place all of his works. This would provide a more adequate experience of the breadth and depth of his artistic skill. Even then, since much of Michelangelo remains unexpressed in his actual achievements, the collective display would provide a still inadequate insight into his genius.

Even more dramatically is it true that the cumulative display of all of God's creatures serves only as the partial, inadequate manifestation of his creativity. It reminds us that he infinitely transcends these achievements, wonderful as they are.

Michelangelo has long been dead. However, his work continues to exist for us to contemplate because he carried it out on materials such as stone, canvas or walls that exist independently of him. While Michelangelo is no longer on earth, his Pieta is still with us because the marble on which he carved it continues to exist. It depends on the artist for its unique shape and form, but not for its existence.

In making a comparison of God's creative work to that of an artist, we should remember Saint Thomas's important qualification. When God acts, unlike Michelangelo who is only the partial cause of his work, he is the total cause. The entire effect of his creativity depends immediately on his sustaining power, like the beam of light coming from the sun. If God removes his sustaining power it will not continue to exist.

THE PRESENCE

When we contemplate the Pieta, we experience the enduring effect of the creative activity of Michelangelo that took place five hundred years ago and then came to closure. When we contemplate God's creatures, we are experiencing something of the ongoing creative activity of God.

Michelangelo is embodied in his work and we experience his presence in that work. However, his is no longer a living, creating presence. God's presence in his creative work is a living, on going, creating, dynamic presence. We are watching God at work as we contemplate the lilies, birds, sunrises and children. Jesus teaches us that not a swallow falls to the ground that does not have its place in the Father's loving plan.[6] When Saint Francis of Assisi contemplated the splendor of Brother Sun rising in the morning, he was experiencing the creative love of the Father in the very act of causing the sunrise.

It is in the context of being attuned to God's living presence, of being enthralled by our Creator's actions in history that Catholics should understand the fascination of going on pilgrimage to holy places. It is not that God, on his part, is more fully present in those places than he is in our homes. It is because God freely chose to manifest his presence in special ways in those parts of the world. Therefore it supports our awareness of God to go to these holy places and experience their unique revelations of his presence.

Consider, for example, the Holy Land. We go there because two thousand years ago God chose on that sacred soil to reveal his presence in a unique way by assuming our human nature and becoming one with us. He did not choose to do this in New York State or in California, but in Israel.

It helps our recollection to go to Bethlehem and Nazareth, to walk along the Sea of Galilee where Jesus walked with his disciples. We sense and experience the divine presence in the garden of Gethsemane where Jesus experienced his anguish. The locations where God reveals his presence in extraordinary ways take on a special significance. The significance is not, of course, because he is more fully there than in any other part of creation.

What is the relative importance of God's presence in our parish churches as distinct from his presence in our homes? What is to be said about the children in their warm beds, protesting the need to go from that warmth into the cold to get to Mass? Our churches are special, sacred places not because God is more fully present there than elsewhere.

We visit our churches because there we encounter the person of the Word of God in the human nature of Christ. Christ's presence in the Eucharist transcends God's presence found in the Holy Land, Lourdes, or other holy places.

For the children in their warm beds protesting the need to go to Mass, the response should be something like this. You are right. God is as fully present in your warm bed as he is in the parish church. But, because Christ has not yet come fully alive in you, you cannot experience his presence. Therefore, we are going to our parish church to encounter the presence of the human nature of Christ. We are going to invite God, acting through the Word made flesh, to bring Christ alive in us more fully. So we will return home, not bringing God with us since he is already here, but bringing a new awareness and responsiveness to his presence through Christ having come more alive in us.

The Eucharist is the extraordinary instrument through which God has chosen to effect the most profound spiritual changes in our lives. It is through the coming alive of Christ in us that we are finally awakened to this omnipresent God.

---

[1] God is transcendent because as creator of the universe he is independent of it and surpasses all creation. Immanence and transcendence must not be looked upon as contraries.

[2] Cf. Thomas Aquinas, *Compendium Theologium* Part One Chap. 102

[3] Rom 11:33-34

[4] Cf. Thomas Aquinas, *Compendium Theologium* Part One Chap. 102

[5] Michelangelo Buonarotti is arguably the greatest artist produced by Western Civilization. There is near universal agreement that he is the supreme artist of the Renaissance. He was born in 1475 and died in Rome in 1564. His seminal works in architecture, painting and sculpture are noted for their humanistic and deeply religious content.

[6] *Cf.* Matt 10:29

CHAPTER THREE

The Awakening

Though God is present we may not be aware
of the divine dimension of our existence

§

Sin impedes our experience of God

§

We sin by turning to God's gifts and seeking
in them the happiness we must seek in God
himself

§

Christ comes to awaken us to God

§

The journey is a lifelong process

§

Christ's human nature is a model for our
journey

§

THE AWAKENING

As noted earlier, Catholic faith in the omnipresence of God calls for two important distinctions in its application to the journey of salvation. We have seen that God is manifested differently in each creature, even though he is fully present to all of them. The second distinction agrees it is true that God is already fully present to us. However, the fact that he is as fully present as ever he will be *on his part* does not mean that we are actually experiencing his presence.

If I were to stand out of doors facing the noonday sun, the light of the sun would be fully present to me. However, if I were blind, I would see nothing. If I were seated in a concert hall where the orchestra was playing a glorious symphony of Beethoven, his great music would be present to me and to all in that hall. However, if I were deaf, I would hear nothing. If someone were to sprinkle on me expensive perfume so that a glorious fragrance surrounded me, the fragrance would be present to me. However, if my olfactory nerves were dead, I would smell nothing. If someone were to brush my fingers against the finest fur or smoothest silk, a wonderful sense experience would thereby be present to me. However, if my fingers were numb, I would feel nothing. If one of the worlds great chefs were to prepare a superb dish for me and invite me to eat, a wonderful savor would be present to me. However, if my taste buds had been destroyed, I would taste nothing.

Let us recall the words of Saint Paul describing God's presence, "In him we live and move, and have our being."[1] According to Saint Paul God is fully present around us and within us.

We are like fish swimming in an ocean of divine love. Unfortunately, we are blind and deaf fish, unable to see and hear his presence. We are unable to taste or feel his presence. We are unable to detect the wonderful fragrance that accompanies his presence.

What impedes our ability to respond to God even though he has been fully present in our lives from the beginning? Jesus informs us that the primary barrier to our experience of God's presence is sin. We sin by turning to his gifts and seeking in them a happiness that only God can provide.

We act as if these precious gifts did not come from him but belong by right to us. Thus we use his gifts to shut him out of our lives. The consequences of sin are spiritual blindness and deafness. Sin destroys the spiritual faculties that would allow us to see, hear, taste, smell and touch his presence.

The symbols of sin in the gospels are precisely such physical disabilities as blindness, deafness and leprosy. These disabilities come with the partial or complete loss of vital responsiveness.

As Jesus went about healing the sick, bringing the dead to life, restoring sight to the blind, granting hearing to the deaf, making the paralyzed mobile, he was teaching us that he has the power to heal our spiritual illnesses. He was teaching us that he has the power to open us to the experience of the Father's presence.

Christ comes, therefore, not to bring God to us or bring us to God, since God is already fully present to us. Christ comes to effect the interior changes in us that will open us to the experience of God's presence. Christ comes to loosen our myopic concentration on the wonderful gifts God has given to assist us on our journey of salvation. As these internal changes take place we gradually become awakened more and more to the presence of God in our lives.

The journey of salvation is not a journey in space but a process of awakening to God's presence. It is a coming alive through Christ to the richness of the creative power of God's love. It is an awakening to a love that was with us from the beginning.

The awakening process stems from a radical transformation of the soul. This transformation is known as sanctifying grace. Sanctifying grace provides for a greater participation in God's life than is possible through human nature in itself.

The growth of sanctifying grace in us entails a complex progression of interior change. Its dynamic growth effects every aspect of our internal lives – our souls, heads, hearts, imaginations and emotions.

Internal spiritual growth has been the object of study and reflection for two thousand years by the inspired writers of the New Testament, the early Fathers of the Church, great theologians and spiritual directors, and mystics and saints. Internal spiritual growth is the object of what is known as moral and spiritual theology. Moral theology examines among other things, the nature of sin, redemptive grace, sacraments, virtues, vices, and the dynamics of prayer.

The model of the spiritual journey of awakening to God is the human nature of Jesus. In His human life we have the clearest, deepest and most complete expression of the harmony necessary between human and divine natures to remove all obstacles to the face to face encounter with God. As Christ grows in us, step by step purifying and reshaping our inner lives into his image and likeness, we progressively awaken to God's presence.

At first we become conscious of God's love around us. Then we become aware of God's love within us. Jesus teaches us that "I am the way, and the truth and the life; no one comes to the Father, but by me." He adds as well, "If you had known me, you would have known my Father also; henceforth you know him and have seen him."[2]

Christ is the unique way of salvation who reveals to us how to come alive to God. We will now seek to learn from the life and teaching of Christ the basic dynamics of the spiritual journey of awakening to God's presence.

---

[1] Acts 17:28
[2] John 14:6-7

CHAPTER FOUR

The Way of Love

Love moves us on the journey of spiritual
awakening

§

Experiencing the love of others requires love
in our own hearts

§

Only saints go to heaven

§

Holiness requires love not extraordinary
phenomena

§

Christ displayed perfect love on the cross

§

Love is possible for each and everyone

§

THE WAY OF LOVE

How do we move along the spiritual journey to the experience of the Father's loving presence? The answer comes through Our Lord's teaching in the gospels. He tells us that "As the Father has loved me, so have I loved you; abide in my love. If you keep my commandments you will abide in my love, just as I have kept my Father's commandments and abide in his love."[1] The way to perfect union with God is the way of love, perfect love.

Common sense tells us that the precondition for experiencing the lovableness of others is the presence of love in our own hearts. Insofar as love is in our hearts we are able to experience, we might say touch, taste, hear, see love in others.

We can be surrounded by love, but if love is not in our hearts we remain blind, deaf and insensitive to its presence in others. Only love in our hearts awakens us to the lovableness around us. And only perfect love can awaken us to the perfect love of God.

God is love: perfect, eternal, infinite, pure love. The face to face encounter with God, then, involves the experience of perfect love. The primary internal change that Christ must effect in us, therefore, is that which makes us capable of experiencing pure love.

In my evangelizing travel from parish to parish I often have the following experience. I arrive in a new parish and meet one of the parishioners. I ask him or her to tell me about the parish. The answer can be, "This parish is the pits, Father. We have no one here but gossips. The people are critical of everyone. Most are power hungry types who try

27

to run everything. Father, you will find little of the loving and lovable in this community."

Asking the same question of another parishioner I can receive an entirely different answer. This person says to me:

> Father, we have wonderful people in this parish. Of course we have our headaches and problems. You cannot get a group of persons together any place without problems. Notwithstanding, we have wonderful people here. You cannot believe the loving service that comes out of the Saint Vincent de Paul Society and the Legion of Mary. Down the block we have this mother of three who is struggling with cancer. Her joy and strength are an inspiration to all of us. Old Joe here is in church daily for hours, praying for the rest of us. Father, I could go on all day boring you with examples of loving persons who inspire us all. Father, there are a lot of loving and lovable people in our parish.

These individuals are telling me about the same group of persons and offering entirely different accounts. Each thinks that he is telling me about the parish community. Each is, of course, telling me about himself. The first person, without realizing it, is telling me that he is a self-centered, unloving person who can see no good in others unless they fit into the narrow world of his preoccupation with self. The second person, unknowingly, is revealing to me that there is a great, generous love in his heart for others. Because of this love he is able to recognize and celebrate the love he experiences in those around him.

To repeat, it is the love in our hearts that allows us to recognize and experience, that is to hear, see, smell, touch, feel and celebrate the love we meet with in others. Absent such love in our hearts we can be surrounded by wonderful, loving and lovable persons but we will remain deaf, blind, and insensitive to the presence of their love. This is true of the love we meet with in this world. It is equally true of the experience of the presence of God's love.

Let me describe another experience I come across. I enter a parish community where everyone points out to me a person I will call Mary. They tell me:

> Father, Mary is the most wonderful person. She is everyone's mother. Your problems are her problems. Your joys are her joys. She is an inspiration to all of us. Sam, her husband, is the luckiest person in the world to have such a loving and lovable wife.

Then Sam comes to me to talk over a problem he has to endure:

> Father, my great cross in life is my wife, Mary. She is a miserable housekeeper. She cannot cook. She cannot even boil water. Every time she takes the car out, I know that it will come back with a dent somewhere on it. I sit there waiting for my dinner while she is off visiting someone in the hospital or someone sick at home. This is my heavy burden, Father.

Poor Sam! Everyone can see the goodness of Mary except him. Sam thinks that he is telling me about his wife. In fact he is telling me about himself. He is revealing to me that there is little love in his heart and so he remains blind and insensitive to the lovableness of his wife which everyone else in the parish sees and celebrates.

Unless Sam becomes a more loving person himself, he will never recognize what others see in Mary. If he cannot recognize and respond to the lovableness of Mary whom he can see, hear and touch, how can he recognize and respond to the invisible presence of divine love. Jesus puts it simply, "If I have told you earthly things and you do not believe, how can you believe if I tell you heavenly things?"[2] If we do not respond to the love we see around us, how can we respond to the love of God that we cannot see?

Recently I offered Mass for a group of elementary Catholic students on the feast of All Saints. The grades ran from the first to the eighth. I began my homily by asking, "How many of you want to become saints?" Three or four hands went up, slowly, and tentatively from the first and second graders. The students from the third grade on up raised not a single hand.

I then asked, "How many of you want to get to heaven?" Immediately every hand in the group was raised with no hesitation whatsoever. Some, in their eagerness to get into heaven, even raised two hands.

I told them, "We have a problem here. To my knowledge, the only way you can get into heaven is by becoming saints. The only 'ticket to heaven' is holiness. Should you all get to heaven, and I pray that all of you will, the only persons you will find there will be saints. If you really want to get into heaven and spend your eternity with those you love, your parents, family and friends, you will have to think seriously about becoming saints."

When persons hesitate to think about becoming saints, it is usually because of a flawed notion of holiness. Many identify holiness with bizarre phenomena, extraordinary mortification, strange mystical experiences, revelations, apparitions, performing miracles, out of the body experiences, prophecy and other equally unusual phenomena.

Holiness essentially has little to do with these extraordinary kinds of things. We come across nothing of this in the life of the Little Flower. What made her a great saint was that she did the ordinary, everyday things of life with an extraordinary love.

We do not read of Mary performing miracles, although at Cana she occasioned one. Apart from two significant dreams, we read nothing about these strange happenings in the life of Saint Joseph. We know that he was a good husband and father. We can assume that he was a good carpenter. No one in the little village of Nazareth suspected anything unusual about the Holy Family.

After observing Jesus closely for thirty years in a small village, no persons were more surprised than the villagers when Jesus began his public ministry. They said, "Is not this the carpenter, the son of Mary"[3]

Jesus tells us that holiness has to do with one essential reality, love. "You shall love the Lord your God with all your heart, and with all your soul, and with all your mind. This is the great and first commandment. And a second is like it. You shall love your neighbor as your self. On these two commandments depend all the law and the prophets."[4]

Let us quote again Jesus' description of the way to salvation "As the Father has loved me, so have I loved you; abide in my love. If you keep my commandments you will abide in my love, just as I have kept my Father's commandments and abide in his love."[5] This is his Father's plan for us. If we are not seriously striving to become saints it means that we are saying, "No" to God's plan.

Holiness means love then, and love is the only way to the face to face union with God. The journey of salvation is primarily an internal journey of transformation of the heart, from imperfect to perfect love. Only through Christ can such a transformation be effected. What is the single, most critical change that Christ must effect in us? Christ comes to take possession of our hearts. He comes to change our heart of stone into one filled with his love.[6]

31

Dying on the cross Jesus teaches us a supremely important lesson about love. We see in him hanging there, a broken, helpless, ineffective human, stripped of everything. He is abandoned by his friends, betrayed by one closest to him, taunted by his enemies, physically immobilized, the symbol of utter impotence. His opponents have successfully taken everything from him except one last possession, the inner freedom to chose how he will react to his tragic plight.

With his last breath he exercises that inner freedom by raising his eyes to heaven and praying, "Father, forgive them; for they know not what they do."[7] He exercised the most perfect act of love that will ever come from a human being. His act of love contained in it the fullness of divine love. His act of love gave birth to divine love in our world in a radically new way.

With that inner exercise of love Jesus overcame the hatred of his enemies, brought victory out of defeat and conquered the world of human sinfulness. His victory opened the door to heaven! The face to face loving union with God, lies open before us!

Jesus on the cross teaches us that it requires nothing to love but a great, generous heart. The essence of holiness is love. You can not plead, therefore, that you are unable to aspire to holiness because you are too poor, too old, too young, physically handicapped, uneducated, illiterate, lacking in social status or influence, untalented, a nobody, alone, emotionally distressed, bereft of artistic ability, ugly, unlovable, a victim of stuttering, afflicted by nervous habits, sick, terminally ill, or frail in other ways.

None of those things have anything to do with your capacity to love. Among the greatest saints you will find persons suffering from all those and other human limitations.

Nor can you plead that you would like to be a more loving person, but others will not allow it. No human has such control over your inner freedom. The only person that has this control and can keep you from growing in love is yourself. If you are not growing in love there is only one explanation. You, yourself, choose not to love. This is the lesson we receive from Jesus on the cross.

If you were to say to me, "Father, this discussion is all well and good but, I find the word 'love' too abstract to understand. What in the concrete is expected of me if I am to become a more loving person? Please provide me with a more detailed map. Help me along this journey of salvation, this transformation of heart that will bring me more and more alive to God's presence." I could find no better source of such an outline than Saint Paul.

Saint Paul tells us all about the anatomy of holiness when he writes, "If I speak in the tongues of men and angels, but have not love, I am a noisy gong or a clanging cymbal. And if I have prophetic powers and understand all mysteries and all knowledge, and if I have all faith so as to remove mountains, but have not love, I am nothing. If I give away all I have, and if I deliver my body to be burned, but have not love, I gain nothing. Love is patient, and kind; love is not jealous or boastful; it is not arrogant or rude. Love does not insist on its own way; it is not irritable or resentful; it does not rejoice at wrong, but rejoices in the right. Love bears all things, believes all things, hopes all things, endures all things."[8]

In these words Saint Paul says it all. He offers us a perfect map to guide us on our journey. Love, is the way, and the only way to the end of the journey of salvation. It is the way to the face to face encounter with the God, who has been with us from the beginning.

[1] John 15:9-10

[2] John 3:12

[3] Mark 6:3

[4] Matt 22:37-40

[5] John 15:9-10

[6] *Cf.* King James Bible Zechariah 7:12 Yea, they made their hearts as an adamant stone, lest they should hear the law, and the words which the LORD of hosts hath sent in his spirit by the former prophets: therefore came a great wrath from the LORD of hosts.

[7] Luke 23:34

[8] 1 Cor. 13:1-7

CHAPTER FIVE

The Three Stages of Awakening

Questions about the journey of salvation

§

Christ's admonition

§

Protestant and Catholic views of the journey

§

In this life we see only reflections of God

§

A study of Christ shows three mirrors of
God in this life

§

The journey of the disciples illuminates our
journey

§

THE THREE STAGES OF AWAKENING

We have seen thus far that the journey of salvation is not a journey in space. It is rather a journey of internal change. Change is effected in us when we become, through Christ, awakened to God's presence and love for us. These conclusions raise a number of questions that must be addressed. These questions include the following:

• Can the awakening to God's presence be instantaneous?

• Can the journey be concluded in this life?

• Does the journey come to an end at death?

• Are there different stages in the awakening process?

• Why must one die to see God face to face?

• What is the face to face encounter with God like?

Let us turn to Saint Paul for further insight into the soul's journey to God. Saint Paul has some good news for us about this journey, and some news that is seemingly not so good. Regarding the latter he tells us that in this life no one sees God face to face.[1]

This means that the end of the journey of salvation is not arrived at until after death. Further, Saint Paul teaches that the journey involves a life time of struggle, continuing up to and including death itself. "With fear and trembling"[2] we must work out our salvation. It will be the runner in the race who perseveres to the end of the race who will win the imperishable crown.[3]

37

When a young man approached Jesus with the question, "How can I achieve union with God?"[4] Jesus could have answered him as he did the good thief on the cross. He could have promised "today you will be with me in paradise."[5] However, Jesus' response was quite different. He said to the young man "You lack one thing; go sell what you have, and give to the poor, and you will have treasure in heaven; and come, follow me."[6]

The young man was seeking instantaneous union with God. This is a natural desire. Nothing is more natural than our desire for quick and easy solutions, answers right here and now. However, Jesus' response is, as it was to the young man, to embark on a long struggle. A struggle that must continue to the end of life itself.

Catholic faith is decidedly different from the understanding of the born again Christian who here and now experiences the certitude of his salvation. According to one Protestant view the experience of a certitude of salvation is the surest sign that one has completely surrendered his life to God. The absence of such certitude of salvation is the sure sign that the individual has not yet experienced the saving embrace of Christ's love. This view answers an intense natural desire. Therefore, it exercises a powerful attraction on everyone who hears it.

The Catholics faith expresses no doubts about Christ's triumph over sin and death, and that his victory makes salvation available to all who turn to him. The effectiveness of Christ's triumph is not in question. At the same time we must be conscious of the reality of our freedom and the very real possibility that we can say "no" to Christ. Think of what Saint Paul tells us "For I do not do the good I want, but the evil I do not want is what I do."[7] The doubts that Catholics have do not relate to Christ, but to human vacillation and weakness of will. Like Saint Paul, we must turn to Christ with supreme confidence in him, but

38

always aware of our weaknesses as we live out our life in 'fear and trembling'.

The desire for assurance of instant salvation is natural and understandable. But there is a danger in such an assurance. It can be an excuse to avoid taking up the cross, the life long struggle that Christ invites us to carry.

It is the sin of presumption to affirm that salvation will be ours irrespective of the way we exercise the God given gift of freedom. Christ comes not to render this freedom irrelevant, but to transform it by gradually taking possession of our hearts. We keep returning to the admonition of Jesus that the kingdom of heaven is like a woman giving birth to a baby, with the travail and struggle inherent in the process.[8] Jesus does not offer a quick and easy end to the struggle.

The good news from Saint Paul is that, while no one sees God face to face in this life, "We are able to see him, obscurely as in a mirror."[9] In this life we cannot see God's face but we can see reflections of his presence.

The journey of spiritual awakening to God's loving presence in this life entails a daily contemplation of his reflections. The mirrors that reflect his presence exercise a profound purification and remaking of our inner being. Our growing consciousness of the reality of these mirrors and our submission daily to their transforming power is the essential condition for our progressive awakening to the divine presence.

The clearest illustration of the nature of the spiritual journey to God is found in the development of relations between Jesus and his followers. We find an outline of the journey in the description of Jesus' mission and the changes he effected in the lives of his disciples that are given in the Gospels. We discover the different stages his followers must pass through. We are also given the clearest hints of what the face to face encounter with God will entail.

THE JOURNEY TO GOD

We will use the spiritual journey of the disciples of Jesus to illuminate our journey to God. This is the journey that Christ invites all of us to undertake, with him as our guide. When we study the words and actions of Jesus in the four Gospels, we can identify through his teaching and example three mirrors through which he radically remolds the inner lives of his disciples.

The first mirror reflecting God's otherwise invisible presence, is the mirror of nature. The lilies of the field, the birds of the air, the miracle of children reflect and make known the divine wisdom, love, beauty and power. Jesus begins the journey by awakening his disciples to the Father's loving presence all around them. He teaches them to see the whole of creation through his eyes and to come alive to the radiance of God's presence.

After awakening in his followers' consciousness of the divine presence shining forth from the works of creation, Jesus then offers his followers a second mirror. This second mirror in an immeasurably more wonderful way reflects the otherwise hidden presence of the Father. This second mirror is the Christ that the disciples see and hear outside of them.

Christ's human nature is the mirror of the divine. Jesus tells his disciples, "I am the way, and the truth and the life; no one comes to the Father, but by me."[10] Gradually, slowly the disciples become awakened to the extraordinary revelation of divine wisdom, love, power, mercy, forgiveness and joy that they are encountering in the words, actions and being of the man they know as The Nazarene.

At the second stage of awareness the disciples are still experiencing reflections of God's presence through mirrors outside them. As yet, they do not encounter reflections of the divine coming from within them through the maturity of Christ's presence within.

The third stage, the mirroring of the divine presence from within, we know as the coming of the Holy Spirit, the

Pentecost event. It is only then that the disciples can say, as Saint Paul later says, "It is no longer I who live, but Christ who lives in me."[11] This represents the third mirror of the divine, and the third stage of the journey of coming alive to God's presence.

These three stages of awakening normally should not be understood to follow in a rigid, logical order. One stage flows into another, but all three can develop simultaneously. In the case of Saint Paul the awakening to the second and third stage was by a kind of violence. On the way to Damascus he was knocked to the ground "And for three days he was without sight, and neither ate nor drank."[12] The awakening can indeed be a sudden and shattering one. Paul speaks of himself as being born to Christ 'out of due time' and, one might say, in an unnatural way.[13]

However, the normal pattern of God's providential plan for our journey of salvation through Christ may be seen in the Gospels. The experiences of Jesus' disciples reflect the reality of what is involved in coming alive to God's presence.

Even with the coming of the Holy Spirit in the third stage, the followers of Christ do not yet see God face to face. They have not yet come to the end of the journey.

What must happen to remove the final barrier that shuts them off from this face to face encounter with the infinite love of the Father? Jesus' teaching about it is unequivocal. They must die. In God's plan only death removes the final barrier.

Death, as Christ witnesses on the cross, is the doorway to heaven. Death is the doorway to salvation, the face to face encounter with the infinite, pure love of God. We will later examine the mysterious role that death plays in this journey, and why each of us must undergo this experience to reach our goal. We will also consider why a

41

final purification must follow physical death to prepare most persons for the face to face encounter with God.

Finally, we will ask what will it be like to see God face to face. What kind of experience will it entail? What will be the accompaniments of this experience? Presupposing we get through that door and arrive where God, our Father intends us to be, how will we spend our eternity?

---

[1] For now we see in a mirror dimly, but then face to face 1 Cor 13:12

[2] *Cf.* Phil 2:12

[3] *Cf.* 1 Cor 9:24

[4] *Cf.* Mark 10:17

[5] Luke 23:43

[6] Mark 10:21

[7] Rom 7:19

[8] *Cf.* John 16: 21

[9] *Cf.* 1 Cor 13:12

[10] John 14:6

[11] Gal 2:20

[12] Acts 9:9

[13] *Cf.* 1 Cor 15:6

CHAPTER SIX

The Mirror of Nature

Christ teaches us to see ordinary things in an
extraordinary way

§

God's work in nature exceeds the greatest
human achievements

§

Mary's faith allowed her to say yes to God

§

The Word of God is the author of nature

§

Saint Francis' experience of nature

§

THE MIRROR OF NATURE

When Jesus began His public ministry and gathered followers to begin with them the journey to the promised land, what did he do? Did he transport them to some distant galaxy where they entered into God's presence? Or did he do something more modest? Did he merely take them to another exotic part of the earth such as the Ganges or Nepal to acquire enlightenment through contact with God's presence in those places?

Jesus did none of these things. He began with them in the Holy Land and ended there. To the best of our knowledge the majority of his followers died in the same place where they first met him. Certainly there was no journey in space involved.

Did Jesus provide his followers with a magic potion, or an exotic psychedelic drug that offered them an experience of the beatific vision? He did not.

Did he lead them in extraordinary ascetic practices, that brought them to deeper levels of self consciousness and awareness of the 'divine' within? On the contrary, the accusations of his critics had to do with the singular lack of any form of asceticism either in him or in his disciples.

Did Jesus as a master of the soul lead his disciples on a psychological journey? Did he lead them through a tortuous descent into the depths of their psyches where they experienced their deeper, truer self with release and bliss? Once again the answer is no.

Did he introduce them to mysterious, ritualistic, mystical practices that effected magical changes within them? Did he induce in them exotic, ecstatic states of consciousness, filled with the Spirit, which brought them to the very threshold of paradise? Jesus did none of these things.

What then did he do to awaken his followers to the experience of God's presence? Jesus' first steps with his followers on the journey of salvation were deceptively ordinary, almost trivial. He started out by inviting his disciples to look around them at the familiar objects they saw every day. He spoke of birds, flowers, little children, bread and water, and the sunrises and sunsets that opened and closed their daily lives. The impression is there was nothing new, nothing unusual. Everything appears all too ordinary.

In the springtime they probably did look with momentary wonder at the freshly blooming flowers. At times birds could exercise a brief fascination. Certainly, particularly beautiful sunrises or sunsets would briefly attract their gaze. At times they would enjoy the beauty of little children before finding their behavior irritating. Beyond these momentary experiences, the whole scene lacked any special significance for them.

Jesus showed them nothing new. All of his teaching dwelt upon the ordinary, old, familiar, everyday things in daily living. He spoke of eating and drinking, sleeping and waking, laughing and crying, giving birth to babies, arguing with family members, planting seeds in the ground, catching fish, collecting taxes. These were the everyday things Jesus spoke of.

What Jesus did, was to change the inner perspective from which they looked out on these familiar objects. He taught them to see the world around them in a radically new way. He assisted them to experience this world as a work of divine art radiating the presence of his Father's love. In a sense he brought them down on their knees before the whole of creation. He taught them, not to worship nature as divine, but to recognize the reflections of the divine in nature.

46

THE MIRROR OF NATURE

The full genius of Beethoven is stamped on each note of his music. Similarly Jesus shows his followers the divine touch in each nuance of nature. The full artistic power of Michelangelo is present in every stroke of his brush and cut of his chisel. Similarly Jesus taught his followers that divine love, wisdom and artistry are manifested in every aspect of the created universe. "Are not two sparrows sold for a penny? And not one of them will fall to the ground without your Father's will. But even the hairs of your head are all numbered."[1]

In this latter example, one suspects that Jesus was planting the seeds of insight in his disciples. They would need to think of the Father's loving plan when later they contemplated the seeming meaningless reality of his dead body hanging from the cross.

We see Jesus' teaching illustrated in the words "Look at the birds of the air: they neither sow nor reap nor gather into barns, and yet your heavenly Father feeds them. Are you not of more value than they? And which of you by being anxious can add one cubit to his span of life?"[2] As his words penetrated ever deeper into their consciousness, there awakened in them a new awareness of the mirroring of divine providence in these workings of nature. Certainly, those who heard Our Lord speak these words could never again look at birds in the same way.

We read further in the gospel of Matthew "Consider the lilies of the field, how they grow: they neither toil nor spin; yet I tell you, even Solomon in all his glory was not arrayed like one of these. But if God so clothes the grass of the field, which today is alive and tomorrow is thrown into the oven, will he not much more clothe you, O men of little faith."[3] From that day forward, never again could his followers contemplate the wild flowers without being reminded of his words and seeing in them a mirror reflecting divine providence at work.

To appreciate the full import of Jesus' teaching about the flowers of the field, one has to remember that for the Jews of his time the richest, wisest, most powerful person who ever existed was Solomon.

As Jesus spoke, the great temple of Solomon still existed in all of its glory.[4] For the Jewish people it was the wonder of the world. Every religious Jew living away from the Holy Land, dreamed of one day going on pilgrimage to Jerusalem and offering sacrifice within the temple of Solomon that housed the 'holy of holies'.

Two thousand years later we can go to old Jerusalem and contemplate the foundation stones still remaining of the great temple of Solomon. We know these stones as the 'wailing wall' that every devout Jew yearns to touch and pray against. If we marvel today at these magnificent remains, imagine the experience of the Jew in Jesus' time who could witness the temple in the fullness of its perfection.

What does Jesus mean when he tells his followers that not even Solomon in all of his splendor could rival the glory of a wild flower that springs up to-day and is gone tomorrow? He is teaching them, among other things, that the lowly wild flower is more a mirror of the divine than the greatest achievements of human creativity.

His message is this; Think of what God the Father can do to you and for you if you allow him to be your God and invite him to fulfill his plan in your life. Think what will happen if you say yes to his plan instead of playing at being God and trying to live out your own dream for yourself.

When Jesus cried "Oh men of little faith" he would not have included his mother, Mary, who had said yes to God's plan. Mary became his mother, when she was a young Jewish girl of thirteen or fourteen years of age, growing up in a tiny, insignificant village in the Holy Land.

She did exactly what Jesus was encouraging his disciples to do through the example of the wild flowers. She said "yes" to God's plan for her. She allowed him to direct and control her life, to shape and form her.

Two thousand years later this Jewish girl has become the best known, most loved and revered of women. She is the inspiration of the greatest architecture, music, paintings, and poetry. She is an example of the wonderful mystery of the nurturing love of God. When the explanation of the phenomenon of Mary is sought, the answer is quite simple. In an admirable embodiment of her son's teaching about the wild flowers, she said "yes" to God's loving plan for her.

Jesus pointed to the lilies of the field and the birds of the air as mirrors of the divine presence. He encouraged his followers to find in them an inspiration to allow the Father's infinite love to mold and form them. We should remind ourselves who it was that said these words. We should ask, whence comes Jesus' masterly insights into the deepest meanings of nature and his ability to set forth authoritatively their role in human life?

We find the answer to these questions in the opening words of the Gospel of Saint John. "In the beginning was the Word, and the Word was with God, and the Word was God... all things were made through him, and without him was not anything made that was made."[5] Therefore, it was through the Word of God that the lilies of the field and the birds of the air were formed and brought into existence.

Finally, we read, "And the Word became flesh and dwelt among us."[6] Jesus is the Word of God through Whom the flowers of the field, the birds of the air and all of nature was created.

When Jesus speaks so illuminatingly and authoritatively about nature, he is speaking about his own loving work. As his followers listen to his words, their experience could be compared to that of one listening to Michelangelo expound on the aesthetic wonders of his Sistine Chapel, or the intricacies of his Pieta. Listening to Michelangelo they would be seeing the Sistine Chapel and the Pieta as they had never seen them before, through the very eyes of their creator. Listening to Jesus they would gain more than an appreciation of the aesthetics of nature. They would discover a revelation of divine love and the divine plan.

His followers began to see through Jesus' eyes the flowers and birds, the sunrises and sunsets, the miracle of little children, and the beauties of nature as he himself saw them. It was as if they were truly seeing them for the first time. They began to experience them as mirrors of the divine, as wonderful revelations of God's love, wisdom, beauty and power. They were awakened to the whole of creation as a work of divine art, more awesome and inspiring than any work of man.

Those who assented to the vision of nature that Jesus shared with his followers experienced a stirring of Faith. The gift of faith embraces a participation in the divine consciousness. Through faith we begin to enter the mind of God, or more accurately, God begins to transform our consciousness. We begin to see as God himself sees. We begin to know as God himself knows. In the gift of Faith we have the seed of the Beatific Vision.

Through this gift of Faith Jesus' followers had reached the first stage of their journey to the face to face encounter with God. He had begun to take possession of their minds.

The saint who most admirably illustrates the awakening to God's presence reflected in nature as a mirror of the divine, is the much loved Saint Francis of Assisi. When ill and close to death, Francis opened the Gospel of Saint Matthew and read there the words of Jesus about the flowers and the birds. He was inspired to respond unconditionally to this message. He made the decision to live henceforth as a flower in the field or a bird in the air, in total, radical dependence on God's providence.

From that moment until the end of his life Francis daily found in nature an ongoing experience of the Father's love actively engaged in the continuing work of creation. Each morning he arose early to witness God bringing about another sunrise. He found it equally important to him to be present in the evening, to experience in the setting of the sun, God concluding another day.

At night Francis saw in the mysterious phases of the moon a living reflection of the unfolding mystery of divine love. He enjoyed preaching to the birds and the flowers, and to fish as well. In the spirit of Jesus' teaching, Francis celebrated the wonders of the whole of nature.

However, he celebrated nature, not as divine, but as the work of God. Francis spoke of Brother Sun and Sister Moon. He did not speak of the sun as a God, or the moon as divine. The sun and moon were wonderful fellow creatures. He rejoiced in experiencing in them reflections of the same divine love that he experienced at the source of his own being.

To find in the beauties and wonders of nature a mirror reflecting the active presence of divine love is, indeed, a precious grace and gift. The journey to God ends here for some. They find in nature their deepest and purest encounter with God's presence. This experience suffices to answer their religious hunger. However, Catholic faith finds in this precious awakening to the divine mirrored in nature, only the first stage in the journey to God.

---

[1] Matt. 10: 29-30

[2] Matt. 6:.26-27

[3] Matt. 6: 28-30

[4] At the time when Jesus spoke Solomon's temple had been rebuilt and enlarged by Herod.

[5] John 1:1-3

[6] John 1:14

CHAPTER SEVEN
The Mirror of Christ Outside

Jesus and the Father are one

§

Jesus' human and divine natures

§

Christ's human nature is a reflection of the
divine

§

The Church is the Mystical Body of Christ

§

THE MIRROR OF CHRIST OUTSIDE

At the Last Supper when Our Lord was speaking intimately to his followers for the final time before his death, he informed them that he would shortly be leaving them to return to the Father. This information deeply disturbed them. Philip asked Jesus "please show us the Father." Jesus answered with disappointment, "Philip, after all this time you still don't understand. When you know me, you know the Father. Philip, don't you realize that when I speak to you, it is the Father who is speaking to you. When you hear me, you hear the Father."[1]

The 'me' that Philip and the others heard, saw, touched and were touched by and with whom they were then breaking bread was obviously the man Jesus. He was the human being with whom they walked daily. His human nature was a finite, created, mortal, human reality, identical with the humanity of his followers. How, then, could Jesus say, referring to his human nature, when you know me, you know the Father? The Father is divine, uncreated, eternal, infinite and immutable.

For the first five centuries of her existence, the Catholic Church struggled to understand more clearly the mystery of the Incarnation. She strove to understand that Jesus was both human and divine, created and uncreated, finite and infinite, mortal and immortal, man and God. As happens to-day, the Church turned for understanding to Jesus' words in Scripture and to the words of other followers taken from the oral tradition.

One of the early heresies in the Church was known as Monophytism.[2] The name derived from the Greek, *monos*, meaning one and *phusis* which means nature.

Monophysitism taught Christ had one nature, one reality possessing human and divine properties. Variants of the doctrine were the human nature is absorbed by the divine, or the divine Second Person of the Trinity disappears in the humanity of Christ or that a unique third nature was created. The Church condemned this and declared solemnly that Jesus was truly human as well as divine, man and God, with each nature distinct from the other while united in the person of the Word.

The Church has consistently affirmed that Jesus was truly, fully human, as human as his followers. It taught that he had a human body, psyche, imagination, memory, intellect and will. As Saint Paul asserted, Jesus is like us in everything but sin.[3]

At the same time the Church has taught that Jesus was truly divine, truly God, eternal, uncreated, immutable, infinite, the perfect being who is the source of all beings. Further, the Church asserted that the human and divine in Jesus were radically distinct. The church taught that the same infinite, qualitative difference that separates humans from the divine, likewise separates the humanity of Christ from his divinity. When the human nature of Christ acted, it was truly a human action, but the person acting was the Word of God. His human acts were instruments of his divine wisdom, power and love.

Finally, the Church affirmed that the Second Person of the Trinity assumed the human nature of Jesus. It was not the Father and not the Holy Spirit, but the Son, the Word of God, who rendered the human nature of Jesus individual and subsistent.

Given this solemn teaching of the Church, what did Jesus mean when he said to Philip "When you know me, you know the Father." How did he equate in himself the human and divine? It may appear that Jesus is guilty of the heresy of the Monophysites condemned at Chalcedon. However, it should be noted that the teaching of the Council of

Chalcedon was arrived at by examining the meaning of these statements of Jesus.

The reflection of the Church was, of course, based on both oral and written traditions. Guided by the Holy Spirit, the following understanding evolved. All the words and actions of Jesus, came from his human nature. That human nature operated as the instrument of his distinct divine nature acting in and through his humanity. Therefore, in the human words and actions of Jesus, the otherwise invisible, intangible, inaudible presence of the divine nature became visible, tangible and audible.

In their experience of the human nature of Jesus acting as the instrument of his separate divine nature, Philip and the other Apostles were seeing, hearing and being touched by the divine. Further, the person they encountered in these human words and actions was the second Person of the Holy Trinity, the Word of God acting through his assumed humanity.

Finally, the presence of that human nature of Jesus involved the immediate, direct presence of God. When Jesus spoke, it was the Word of God speaking. When Jesus reached out and touched them through his genuinely human touch, it was the Word of God touching them. When they experienced the very human acts of love of Jesus, they were experiencing a human love suffused and transformed by divine love made visible, tangible and audible through his human nature. The Person loving them was the Word of God. Any contact with the human reality of Jesus placed his followers in a direct, unmediated, personal encounter with the Word of God.

Let us imagine Jesus speaking intimately with Philip in response to Philip's plea "show us the Father." Imagine Jesus' words describing what we now know through the inspiration of the Holy Spirit and the teaching of the Church.

Philip, do you remember the time you saw me reach out my hand and touch the diseased flesh of the leper, instantly healing that flesh? Did you not realize, Philip, that my human touch, as human, has no more healing power than does your own touch. The divine touch, of course, possesses such healing power. When I chose to reach out my hand, I did so as the instrument of the healing power present in my divine touch. Philip, when I touched that leper, the Father was touching him with all the power present in His touch.

Philip, do you remember the night we were out on the boat and I was asleep? Suddenly a fierce storm came. In fear, you awakened me. My first words to you were what little faith you have. I then commanded the waves to be calm and the winds to be still. Instantly, upon my command, the storm ceased.

Philip, my human will does not have the power to control the elements anymore than your will does. The Father's will has this power. However, I acted as the conscious instrument of the divine will of the Father acting in and through my human will. Therefore, there was present in my human command the very power over the elements uniquely proper to the divine will.

Philip, do you remember the time we found ourselves in a crowded room and the friends of a paralyzed man lowered him through the roof on a litter? Everyone in that room saw a man who was physically paralyzed. I, on the contrary, saw a man who was spiritually and emotionally paralyzed, bitter, full of self pity, angry, envious of others, shut up in himself and incapable of love for others. This is sin.

Sin is a paralysis of the inner spirit. I was more concerned, therefore, with his spiritual paralysis than with the physical. So I said to him, your sins are forgiven. With that act of forgiveness, a wonderful change took place in him. For the first time in years, he experienced a peace and joy within, the absence of fear and guilt, and movements of love and hope. This is the effect on the soul of God's forgiveness. It frees the sinner from spiritual and emotional paralysis. It brings back life and mobility to the spirit.

The Scribes and Pharisees who were present, immediately cried, "blasphemy, blasphemy only God can forgive sins." You know, Philip, they were correct. Sin is an offense against God, and only God can forgive such an offense.

Where they erred, however, was in their failure to recognize in my human act of forgiveness the presence of divine forgiveness. I chose to make my human act of forgiveness the instrument of the divine, acting in, through and with my human forgiveness.

To show them that I possessed such power, as you recall, Philip, I turned to them and said, which is easier to say, your sins are forgiven or take up your bed and walk. To show that the Son of Man has the power to forgive sin, spiritual paralysis, I healed his physical paralysis. Philip, do you still fail to recognize that when I forgive, it is God forgiving.

Jesus' followers grew in awareness of the true meaning of his human words and actions. They recognized in the presence of Jesus a revelation of the divine presence and action. His followers gradually came to see that they were encountering in him a mirror reflecting the divine. With this awareness, they reached the second stage of their journey to the face to face encounter with God.

The first mirror of the divine is nature when seen through the eyes of Jesus. As wonderful as are the reflections of God's presence in the lilies of the field, the birds of the air, the miracle of little children, far more wonderful are the reflections of divinity that we encounter in the human nature of Christ. No part of creation more wonderfully reflects the wisdom, love, beauty, joy and power of God than does the human nature of Christ as the Way, the Truth and the Life.

The grace of Christian Faith is necessary for one to recognize in the human nature of Christ this second mirror of the divine. Without this gift, Jesus is no more than a unique historic person. Without it one will not recognize that he is the Son of God. With the gift of Christian Faith one acknowledges Jesus is the Word made flesh, and the perfect mirror of the divine. It is only those persons graced with this awareness who reach the second stage of the journey to God.

When did Jesus' followers awaken to the full reality of the Incarnation? How did the disciples come to see a mirror of the divine in Christ's humanity? Scholars argue about how and when this took place. While these are interesting and important questions, the question of vital interest to us is, what is the relevance of the Incarnation in regard to *our* journey to God?

THE MIRROR OF CHRIST OUTSIDE

Two thousand years have passed since Jesus walked the earth. Unlike the disciples of Jesus before the Ascension, we can no longer see the human nature of Christ. We cannot hear his human voice speaking to us, or experience His human words of forgiveness. Christ in his human nature, as a second and more perfect mirror of divinity, moved his followers along the journey to God. Are we left only with the first mirror, that of nature, and a record of Jesus' words and actions in the Gospels? According to the teaching of Catholic Faith this is not the case. The human nature of Christ is still accessible to us as it was to his followers two thousand years ago.

The resurrected Christ told his disciples, "All authority in heaven and on earth has been given to me. Go therefore and make disciples of all nations, baptizing them in the name of Father and of the Son and of the Holy Spirit, teaching them to observe all that I have commanded you; and lo, I am with you always, to the close of the age."[4]

---

[1] *Cf.* John 14:8-11

[2] These and other variants were all were condemned at the Council of Chalcedon in 451 AD

[3] *Cf.* 2 Cor 5:21

[4] Matt. 28:16-20

61

CHAPTER EIGHT

The Catholic Way

The faith of Catholics and Non-Catholics

§

Christ is accessible through the sacraments

§

Christ is alive in the world through his
Mystical Body

§

An example of finding the Catholic Faith

§

THE CATHOLIC WAY

I am frequently asked by concerned persons to explain the difference, if any, between Catholic faith and non-Catholic, Christian faith. The question is often like one of these: "are not all Christians really the same?" or "do not all Christians believe in and depend on the same Christ?" or "is Christ not the same for all of his followers?"

My response is both yes and no. While all true Christians believe in the same Christ, they do not locate him in the same place nor experience him in the same way.

Certainly, all true Christians, believe that Christ is both God and man. They believe he was miraculously conceived of a virgin through the power of the Holy Spirit.

Also all true Christians hold that Christ lived some thirty years on the earth, and spent the final years of his life in public activity, teaching and preaching the good news of salvation. They affirm that during his public life he went about ministering to human needs. He attended especially to the needs of the sick and the poor. He worked many miracles in support of his teaching. Christians accept that he developed a community of devoted followers who accepted him as the Messiah.

Christians also accept the truth of the Gospel account that he was put to death by his enemies and three days later, physically arose from the tomb. Note that the bodily resurrection of Christ and his triumph over death have been denied from the beginning, even by persons claiming to be his followers. We find this in the epistle of Paul to the Corinthians.[1]

The denial of the bodily resurrection of Christ, then, is not unique to the contemporary world. However, its affirmation has been one of the signs of authentic Christian faith from the beginning of Christianity.

Finally, all true Christians accept as fact that the resurrected Christ spent forty days after his resurrection in preparing his followers for the next phase of their ministry. After that came the Ascension of the resurrected Christ.

The Ascension of Christ into heaven is the fork in the road where Catholic Christians and non-Catholic Christians differ. For most non-Catholic Christians, Christ is no longer present here on earth.

For many non-Catholics Christ continues to observe us from the heavens and exercises a loving care directing our lives. In particular, he continues to exercise an influence in their lives when they prayerfully contemplate his teachings in the gospels and in sacred scripture. They no longer see Jesus here on earth reaching out to us through his human nature. They no longer experience him speaking to us from a human body. No longer is he forgiving their sins through human acts of forgiveness that they can hear and in which they take an active part. No longer is he sitting at the table with them in his human nature and breaking bread with them.

In the view of many non-Catholics, our experience of Christ is totally different from the one enjoyed by his followers two thousand years ago. When two or three come together in his name he certainly is present in their midst. But they believe that he essentially acts on us from without and from above.

Opposed to this understanding is the Catholic conviction that Christ never left us. The accessibility of Christ to Catholics is through his Mystical Body, the Church. Catholics experience him still fully alive and active on earth as he was two thousand years ago. They can still hear him, see him, walk with him, break bread with him and do all that Philip and his disciples did with him before his Ascension. Simply put, for Catholics the Church is Christ. In the Church he is fully alive and active in this world in both his humanity and divinity.

The significance of the Sacraments is that they make Christ in both his human and divine natures accessible to us. Through them Christ continues to pour the waters of Baptism on us and forgive our sins. He continues to offer his life for us on the cross through the Mass. He feeds us with his body and blood in the Eucharist just as he nourished His disciples.

Christ calls the Holy Spirit down upon us through Confirmation. He empowers us to be loving instruments of his presence through the Sacraments of Holy Orders and Matrimony. Recall Saint Paul's words "Husbands, love your wives, as Christ loved the church and gave himself up for her..."[2]

As the spouse of the Church, Christ would never abandon those whom he loves. He is present to us in the final stages of life with the grace that allows us to surrender our life peacefully back to God through the Sacrament of the Sick.

The Christ that Catholics know and experience is the Christ we encounter fully alive and active in his Mystical Body. For Catholics there is no other Christ. We encounter him in the love of our parents and friends. We encounter him in believing lay persons, priests and religious. We encounter him in the Church's worship. We encounter him in the saints, scholars and spiritual authors. We encounter him in the two thousand year history of his embodiment in the creeds, apostolic activities and magisterial teachings of his Church. It is there that we see him, hear him, touch him and are touched by him.

Even in the inspired writings of Sacred Scripture our experience of Christ presupposes his living presence. He shares himself with us through the collective memory of his words and actions.

No Sacrament more perfectly exemplifies the ongoing, sanctifying presence of the human nature of Christ in this world than the Holy Eucharist. Catholics celebrate in the Eucharist the physical presence of the human nature of Christ. They celebrate the presence of his body and blood, soul and divinity. They celebrate his offering of himself daily on the altar in that same unending, uninterrupted eternal act of perfect love which he initiated on the cross. Through this act of love he continues to give birth in a radically new way to divine love in this world.

This is why Catholics make their children leave their warm beds and usher them out into the cold to participate in the Mass. They do not deny that the omnipresent divinity of Christ is already present to their children in those warm beds. However, they also know that their children will never be awakened to the fact of that presence unless they encounter the human nature of Christ. They know the Eucharist is the instrument through which God has chosen to awaken them to that presence.

Jesus said:

> Truly, truly I say to you, unless you eat the flesh of the Son of man and drink his blood, you have no life in you; he who eats my flesh and drinks my blood has eternal life, and I will raise him up at the last day...He who eats my flesh and drinks my blood abides in me, and I in him[3]

Catholic faith affirms that this Christ is still fully alive in our world. It finds in his Mystical Body the same mirror reflecting divinity that his disciples encountered in the human reality of Christ two thousand years ago.

THE CATHOLIC WAY

All true Christians, indeed, believe in the same Christ and look for salvation through the same Christ. However, all Christians do not locate this Christ in the same place. All Christians do not experience His healing presence in the same way.

An example of Catholic faith, as distinct from Christian faith, is found in the account of the spiritual awakening in the life of Malcolm Muggeridge[4]

Malcolm Muggeridge, influenced by his father, was a very resolute Fabian socialist in his younger years.[5] In a pattern typical of many thinking persons of his era he became enamored of Soviet Russia. When the opportunity arose, he emigrated to Russia. However, unlike many of the influential Socialists of his time, his commitment to truth overcame his impassioned pledge to the Russian regime. Malcolm unflinchingly reported the cruel horrors of Russia under the Communists.

This commitment to speak the truth became Malcolm's badge of distinction. In his work as a newspaper man, magazine editor, television reporter, and television personality he was noted for penetrating analyses. The scrutiny he delivered was notably not attuned to popular opinion and unfailingly critical of established institutions. His ability to say 'the emperor has no clothes' endeared him to audiences worldwide.

In his first job he was a teacher at a Church of England school. Probably as a result of his friendship with a priest there, he became fascinated with the person of Jesus Christ. At first he perceived him, not as divine or the Son of God, but as a wonderful human being.

In his older years he underwent a spiritual awakening. He became convinced that Jesus was indeed the Son of God. He made the decision to surrender his life to the loving care of Jesus and strive to live it in imitation of his example.

However, the Christ he chose to follow was the Christ who no longer lived here on earth. He was the Christ who now dwelt only in the heavens. Malcolm looked around him at the Christian churches, including the Catholic Church, and was decidedly unimpressed by what he saw.

In none of the churches could he detect any evidence of the living presence of Christ. So, he described himself as an un-churched Christian, a Christian who was a member of no church, yet a true disciple of the Christ he encountered in the Gospels. Malcolm continued for a number of years in this form of Christian faith.

In his work for the BBC (British Broadcasting Corporation) he was asked to interview a little known nun; Mother Teresa of Calcutta. He was fascinated by her. He arranged to produce a documentary about her work in Calcutta.

In Calcutta he spent a great deal of time with her. He observed as keenly as possible everything about her. As an artist, he wished to get inside the 'head' and 'heart' of Mother Theresa to find out what really made her 'tick'. The more intensely he studied her, the more convinced he became that she could only be explained by the fact that Christ was truly alive in her. So he came to believe in the living presence of Christ in at least one person on earth.

His faith later grew to recognize the presence of the living Christ in others of heroic virtue. He began to identify Christ at work in missionaries and holy lay persons. He found that unlike other great figures in history who were now dead, Christ was a living presence in modern times.

In time too he came to recognize the living presence of Christ in the institution of the Catholic Church. This is how Malcolm, the un-churched Christian in later years became the Catholic Christian.

This account illustrates how the grace of Catholic faith is received when one recognizes and accepts the reality of Christ's presence in the fullness of his humanity and divinity in his Mystical Body, the Church. Catholic Christian faith is precisely faith in the immanence of Christ in his Church. The object of Catholic Christian faith is the Christ that never left this world. He continues as the groom. He continues to be wedded to his spouse, the community of his followers.

It is this gift of Catholic faith that brings one into the second stage of the journey to God. This faith makes it possible, for those so gifted, to discern with varying degrees of clarity the omnipresent God reflected in the wonderful mirror of the Mystical Body of his Son. This gift allows for a seemingly unlimited variation in the degree in which God's reflected presence can be discerned.

For some the reflection of God's presence in the Church is weak and scarcely discernible. For others the intensity of reflections of God's presence mirrored in his Church is so great that it overwhelms them and threatens to consume them. These are the saints, the holy ones in our midst, whose heads and hearts are filled with the consciousness of Jesus' presence in his Church. Like Mother Teresa, they go about telling everyone in one way or another "do something beautiful for Jesus." Those who reach the second stage of the journey have a growing consciousness of God's presence reflected in Christ's Mystical Body.

The presence of Christ in the Eucharist is the center of their lives. Devotion to his Eucharistic presence is the clearest measure of the intensity of their faith. It is the measure likewise, of how far advanced they are in their journey to God.

In this second stage the encounter with God is still with his presence outside of them. This was true of Christ's disciples also. The disciples who had not yet reached the third stage could not look inside themselves and find there a third mirror reflecting God's presence from within.

71

THE JOURNEY TO GOD

[1] 1 Cor. 15:12

[2] Eph 5:25

[3] John 6:53-57

[4] Malcolm Muggeridge was an English journalist and lecturer He was a very well known figure as editor of the *Punch* magazine renowned for its humor and brilliant satire on politics and social issues. In 1971 he published a book on Mother Teresa titled *Something Beautiful for God.* In 1979 he wrote a book, autobiographical in nature, titled *Jesus Rediscovered.*

[5] Much of what follows is contained in his biography: *Muggeridge: the biography*, Richard Ingrams, Harper San Francisco 1995

CHAPTER NINE
The Mirror of Christ Within

Christ comes to bring us more abundant life

§

God in his love for us shares His divine life
with us as fully as possible

§

Sanctifying grace enables us to respond to
God

§

Christ as an inner presence

§

THE MIRROR OF CHRIST WITHIN

Jesus made two promises to his followers. First, he promised them that he would never leave them. He also promised that his presence would place them into a new, deeper contact with the Father.

At the Last Supper, however, he seemed to contradict these promises. First he informed his followers, to their consternation, that shortly he would leave them to return to the Father. He then informed them of the strange reason for this departure. He said, "Nevertheless I tell you the truth: it is to your advantage that I go away, for if I do not go away, the Counselor will not come to you; but if I go I will send him to you."[1] His presence is depicted as a barrier, an obstacle, to the coming of the Holy Spirit.[2] How is one to reconcile these seemingly contradictory promises?

Before dealing with these puzzling questions, let us briefly review what we have seen so far about the journey to God. First, we saw that this journey is not a spatial one because God is omnipresent. Rather it is a journey of interior change, of coming alive to God's presence. It involves an awakening to God's presence where it has always been, around us and within us.

Christ does not come to bring us to God, or to bring God to us. If God were not already present to us, we would not exist. Christ comes to effect internal changes in us that awaken us in a gradual process to God's presence. Christ comes to enter into and come alive in us. Through his living presence in us we experience the Father's presence in and through him.

We also saw, that no one in this life comes face to face with God. As Saint Paul tells us, we can only see reflections of Him obscurely as in a mirror.

We then identified three mirrors reflecting the divine presence. These three mirrors act to produce change within us. First, there was the mirror of nature when seen through the eyes of Jesus. Secondly, in the human nature of Christ experienced outside us, we find a still more wonderful reflection of the divine.

The third stage is sometimes referred to as the Pentecost Event. With the coming of the Holy Spirit, Christ comes alive in us providing a mirror of the divine within.

To understand this third stage of the journey to God, we must grasp better what is meant by saying that Christ seeks to come fully alive in us. Repeatedly in Christ's teaching we come upon this notion of Christ coming alive in his followers, bringing God alive in them.

The references to this new life through Christ are many. The life giving presence of Jesus is given in "I am the vine and you are the branches..."[3] And "I have come that they may have life..."[4] And "If you knew the gift of God...he would have given you living water..."[5] In particular Jesus admonishes us "unless you eat the flesh of the Son of man and drink his blood, you have no life in you..."[6]

The divine life is described in the Gospels with "The kingdom of heaven is like a grain of mustard seed which a man took and sowed in his field."[7] We see also "Other seeds fell on good soil and brought forth good grain ..."[8] The analogy of the seed reminds us that the divine life is given to us in a form which must be cared for and brought to maturity.

Clearly we need the presence of the Holy Spirit. Jesus says, "unless one is born of water and the Spirit, he cannot enter the kingdom of God..."[9]

Most of Jesus' miracles relate to his life giving power. Sin is presented as the absence of life. The absence of the fullness of life in the leper, the mute, the man who is blind, the paralytic and the corpse are offered as symbols of sin. Jesus' power to restore health and life supports his claim to be able to impart divine life.

Saint Thomas identifies Christ's intention to bring himself alive in his followers as the essence of love. He teaches that love seeks the union of the beloved with the lover.[10]

We love insofar as we seek to bring alive in our beloved the best of what is alive in us. True lovers seek to share the best of what is alive in them, their thoughts, affections, emotions, memories, dreams and their very being. The intent of love is the transformation of the beloved into the image and likeness of the lover. This is true of human love, which is a pale reflection of divine love. It is also true of divine love.

Saint Thomas teaches that the Father in his love for us, seeks to share with us as fully as our human nature allows, his own divine life. This is the purpose of the Incarnation.

Saint Thomas puts it beautifully in speaking of the Incarnation, "God became man in order that man might become like God."[11] Many believe that our human desire to be like God is the essence of sin. But Catholic theology does not see that desire as sinful.

The hunger to share in God's life is planted in us by God with our very nature. Sin does not consist in the desire to be like God. It is rooted in our efforts to satisfy our God hunger in something other than God. It involves seeking a god likeness in ourselves or the created order.

God in his love of humanity desires to see humans elevated to a likeness to his divine nature. In the Incarnation wherein the Word of God assumes our human nature, we find the clearest revelation of this intent of divine love.

God's love for us is infinite. The only limit to this sharing of His life with us comes from our human choices or from limitations inherent in human nature's capacity to be elevated to the divine. The goal of divine love is that all humans might repeat the words of Saint Paul, "It is no longer I who live, but Christ who lives in me..."[12]

Catholic theology explains the love dynamic, of the transformation of human nature into the likeness of God. It identifies the most radical change effected in human nature as taking place in the deepest part of the soul. This change is called sanctifying grace.

Sanctifying grace is defined as the formal participation in the very life of God as God. Its presence and development is the key to understanding the journey of the soul to the face to face, loving union with God.

Sanctifying grace cannot be directly experienced by the person receiving it. It can not be perceived by the senses. However, its presence can be indirectly recognized by the dynamic changes accompanying it in the soul. These alterations occur in the various faculties or powers of the soul such as the intellect, will, emotions, memory and imagination. These changes are called supernatural virtues.

The three most important changes are the theological virtues. These virtues dispose the faculties of intellect and will to relate directly to God. They have God as the object of their activity. They are identified as Faith in the intellect, and Hope and Charity in the will.

Through Faith, Christ enters into and comes alive in our minds. It equips us with the power to assent with certitude to the divine mysteries of revelation.

Hope and Charity in the heart or will introduce a new response to God to bring us to loving union with Him. Most importantly they engender in us a loving hunger and attraction for God. They allow an actual participation in the very love that unites Father, Son and Holy Spirit in the Trinity.

THE MIRROR OF CHRIST WITHIN

Sanctifying grace in the soul and the theological virtues in the intellect and will, alter the powers of the soul in other ways. They prepare the soul to relate to the whole of created reality in a way that furthers its advance to the face to face union with God. These other dynamic dispositions are the supernatural moral virtues. These virtues equip us to make choices in harmony with the hunger for God engendered in us through sanctifying grace.

Admittedly, this is a dry, abstract reflection on the classic Catholic theology of grace and the virtues. However, it serves to put us into contact with the speculative fruit of centuries of meditation on the words of Christ and his mission.

Normally the transforming effects of God's love take place gently and gradually in the soul. Most persons undergoing them are not conscious of the changes taking place. As already mentioned, we do not experience sanctifying grace directly.

Although normally the soul is transformed gradually, sometimes the changes may be sudden and violent. On occasion they are so violent as to leave one painfully aware of their explosive character.

We saw already that this was the case with Saint Paul and his spiritual awakening on the road to Damascus. His encounter with Christ was accompanied by violent internal changes that left him blind and paralyzed for days. This is why he can describe himself as having been born violently and out of due time.[13]

However, Paul's conversion seems to be an exception. In most cases these inner transformations of grace are so gentle, gradual and subtle that they escape our awareness.

Our minds tend to focus more on external reality than on what is going on in our inner world. It is only when contact with outer reality painfully breaks down that a focus on our inner life comes to the foreground of our consciousness. Jesus' disciples also only came to concentrate on the inner life through painful events in their outer world.

From their very first contact with Jesus his followers, without knowing it, became profoundly changed persons. As they followed him from place to place, listening to his words, observing his actions, their inner transformation continued.

In his interaction with the disciples Jesus planted seeds of the divine life in their heads, hearts, emotions, memories and imaginations. During this time Christ was coming alive in them but they were not conscious of these changes. From the first encounter, Jesus in His love for them, began to transform them into his image and likeness

On occasion they certainly recognized signs of changes going on within. They must have been surprised at times to find themselves acting in ways quite different from their past behavior. They made decisions that they would never have made before meeting Jesus. They did things quite differently. We imagine family members and friends must have pointed this out to them.

However, their primary focus remained on what was going on in the world outside them and not on their inner world. Their attention in particular remained fixed with fascination on Jesus and his activities taking place in that outer world.

After two years or more of discipleship, these inner changes had become substantial. It was then time for Jesus to move them along to the next stage in their journey.

Several times during His public ministry we read that Jesus' enemies sought to seize and kill him. Each time they failed because his time had not yet come. Jesus did not allow his enemies to overcome him until the inner transformation of his disciples had reached the degree of maturity that would allow them to survive the trauma of his crucifixion.

THE MIRROR OF CHRIST WITHIN

The opening of the third stage of the disciples' journey began at the Last Supper. To their consternation, Jesus told them that he would leave them before long. Shortly after Jesus was seized by soldiers in the garden, placed on trial, tortured and then crucified. It was then that his disciples fled in fear. Their whole world collapsed around them. It was during the hours following the seizure of Jesus and his death that the disciples suddenly became painfully aware of their inner world. They felt a fear and hopelessness within, the like of which they had never experienced.

Until that time they concentrated on Jesus outside of them. His preaching and teaching; drawing huge crowds; walking on water; performing miracles; filled them with faith in him. His seemingly invincible behavior gave them courage, joy, and enthusiastic expectations of the future.

His external presence brought alive the best in them, noble desires and great dreams. His fame and success also awakened false expectations in them. They argued among themselves as to who would be first when he took over His kingdom.

After his arrest, they witnessed a very different Jesus outside of them. A defeated, beaten, brutalized, helpless Jesus. Finally they saw Christ dead, nailed to the tree of the cross. All the noble dreams in their inner world died with his death.

It was a total collapse of the best within them. Christ died as surely within them as he died physically on the cross. This death state within continued for three days following his burial. When they looked within themselves or at each other, they found no reflections of the divine shining forth. They experienced only memories of cowardice and despair. When they looked at Peter, weeping his bitter tears, they found even less of a mirror of the divine in his pathetic rejection of Jesus.

Three days later when the resurrected Christ stood in their midst, his living, external presence once again brought alive within them wonder, joy, renewed hope and confidence. Their faith was stronger than ever. Christ outside them, mirroring God's presence, brought Christ alive within them again.

During the subsequent forty days Christ frequently reappeared to them. He continued to grow in them through his presence outside, keeping alive in them joy and new expectations.

At the end of forty days the resurrected Christ, in the presence of his followers, withdrew his external presence and ascended into heaven. This time there was no violence or trauma in his departure. They now knew that they were still under his loving protection. He had not abandoned them.

Their joy in his triumph over death and his enemies, was still with them during the following days. In that period they prepared themselves for the next stage of their journey, the coming of the Holy Spirit.

What happened on that first Pentecost? Scripture informs us that they had gathered in the upper room. Suddenly the room filled with winds and tongues of fire descended upon them with the coming of the Holy Spirit. This is a description of what happened outside them, but not what happened within.

Did they undergo an inner experience of coming alive unlike anything they had known previously? I would argue that what they experienced within was something quite familiar. The stirrings of strong faith, courage, wisdom, joy and love were the same inner movements that they had often experienced before when Christ was present outside of them. These were the virtues that came alive in them when they could see, hear and touch Jesus. These were the feelings produced by his triumphant external presence.

Yet now he was no longer standing there outside of them. Notwithstanding that, they experienced his transforming presence in an incredibly heightened way within.

Then the realization came to them. He was still with them. He had not left them. He had only changed the mode of his presence. His presence now was an inner one. He had come to full life within them. Then they could say as Saint Paul said, "It is no longer I who live, but Christ lives in me."[14]

With this coming alive in the Holy Spirit, they entered into the third stage of the journey. They experienced within themselves the fullness of Christ's presence. The mature Christ within, through the gift of the Holy Spirit, was shining forth glorious emanations of divine life.

With their rebirth in Christ, these men who a short time before had abandoned Christ, opened the door of the upper room and issued forth joyfully. The same Peter who denied with an oath even knowing him becomes the fearless leader.

As instruments of Christ's transforming presence within, they begin to preach the good news of the resurrected Christ to an astonished audience. They continued Christ's mission on earth. They proclaimed his message without compromise. They healed the sick, forgave sinners, cared for the poor and abandoned and tirelessly tended to the physical and spiritual needs of others. They attacked the hypocrisy of the Scribes and Pharisees.

They provided to all the same experience of God's presence that they had encountered in Christ. With this, the Mystical Body of Christ, the Church, was born into the world.

The mirror of the living Christ within them did not render unnecessary or meaningless their encounter with the other reflections of God's presence. The mirror of nature and the mirror of Christ's presence in others which they had known were still necessary. They continued to see, with even greater, clarity reflections of God's presence in the lilies of the field, the birds of the air and in little children.

They also came to an entirely new consciousness of Christ's presence in each other. They now saw each other as children of God, made in his image and likeness, and destined for the face to face encounter with God.

They were conscious of Christ's presence in others as individuals, such as Mary, and the other disciples. In particular, this rebirth of Christ within them, heightened their appreciation of the love of Christ that bound them together as a community.

While they experienced different aspects of Christ's presence within different individuals, they were acutely aware that it was only in the community as a whole that they encountered the fullness of Christ's presence. So they prized each individual for the way in which he or she added to their experience of Christ.

---

[1] John 16:7

[2] The *Catechism of the Catholic Church* says "The seven gifts of the Holy Spirit are wisdom, understanding, council, fortitude, knowledge, piety, and fear of the Lord. They belong in their fullness to Christ...They make the faithful docile in readily obeying divine inspirations. CCC 1831

[3] John 15:5

[4] John 10:10

[5] John 4:10

[6] John 6:53

[7] Matt 13:31

[8] Matt 13:8

[9] John 3:5

[10] *Cf.* Thomas Aquinas *Summa Contra Gentiles* Book 1 Chap 91

[11] *Cf.* Thomas Aquinas *Summa Theologiae* Third Part Q 28

[12] Gal 2:20

[13] *Cf.* 1 Cor 15:8

[14] Gal 2:20

CHAPTER TEN

The Coming of The Holy Spirit

Purification

§

Withdrawal of external support initiates
interior growth

§

The greatest intensity of human love

§

Characteristics of the third stage of the
journey

§

THE COMING OF THE HOLY SPIRIT

The Pentecost event brings us to the third stage of the journey to God in this world. There is much discussion today about the proper understanding of the coming of the Holy Spirit. I have met charismatic Catholics who, I have no doubt, have reached the third stage in the journey to God

However, the inner life of a human being is complicated. The stirrings of religious hunger within take on an infinite variety of forms. It is all too easy to attribute to the Holy Spirit inner movements that should be attributed solely to the human spirit. We can best learn from the first Pentecost how the Holy Spirit comes into our lives.

We have seen that the disciples had come through Jesus' eyes to see that nature reflected the Father's presence. Also after some time they had begun to recognize dimly that Jesus was more than merely human. However, it is clear from the Gospel accounts that they still had a long road of spiritual growth ahead. They had to be purified further before they would arrive at the stage in which they experienced the mature presence of Christ within them. It was only after a profound, extremely painful purification that they finally reached the third stage.

It involved a purgation of all false illusions about themselves, a death to self in order to come alive to Christ. They had to experience who and what they truly were without Christ alive in them. They had to experience, as often happens, that the 'old man' in them had killed that living presence of Christ. It was only after this purification had taken place, and they had been emptied of self, that the mature Christ was born in them with the coming of the Holy Spirit.

We find in the person of Saint Peter the clearest example of the dynamics of the transition from the second to the third stage of the journey. Peter's experience illustrates the transition from consciousness of Christ as the mirror of the divine outside, to consciousness of the mature Christ reflecting God's presence within.

Peter heard with amazement at the Last Supper Our Lord's words "Truly, truly I say to you, the cock will not crow, till you have denied me three times."[1] Peter's surprise came not because he learned that he would deny Jesus. In his judgment of himself, such behavior was simply impossible for him. It came rather from the thought that Jesus did not really know him, that Jesus could think him capable of such an action. Peter was deeply hurt. He the loyal, courageous, outspoken Peter a betrayer? Impossible! So Peter uttered those confident words, "Though they all fall away because of you, I will never fall away."[2]

Jesus loved Peter in a special way, and was preparing him for an extraordinary role in the future mission of his Church. Because of this he then turned to him and said, "This very night, before the cock crows, you will deny me three times."[3] Peter, once again, flatly denied the possibility. "Even if I must die with you, I will not deny you."[4]

Imagine what would happen if one were to take Peter aside at that moment and ask him how he could be so certain of his loyalty? He could legitimately point out that during the previous three years he was the most outspoken in his defense of Jesus. He could point out that he had, many times, put his life on the line in his unconditional identification with Jesus.

Imagine if one were to pursue the issue further by challenging Peter. Surely there were times when you wavered, when you experienced doubts about Jesus' mission, when you experienced fear coming from your association with him? Peter, honest person that he was, would probably have acknowledged that there were such

88

moments. But he would have claimed that those moments were aberrations. That the real Peter was that part of him that was loyal, believing, courageous, self sacrificing and true.

Peter would have been partially correct. These qualities were indeed in him. He had been loyal, brave and trustworthy. But, he failed to recognize that the source of these sterling qualities in him came from Christ alive in him. He was experiencing in that part of himself the living Christ within. He had identified the real Peter with that same Christ in him. So, he was surprised and hurt at the words of Jesus.

Later in the evening when Jesus is seized in the garden who is the one who springs to his defense? It is, of course, the loyal, courageous Peter. He takes his sword in hand and cuts off the ear of one of the servants taking hold of Jesus. He probably looked at Our Lord with hurt in his eyes saying, "See. How could you have doubted me?"

A short time later we find Jesus in the courtyard, being brutalized by the Roman soldiers. The other disciples had abandoned Jesus in fear. Again, we find Peter present, loyal to the end. As he watches the cruel treatment of Jesus unfold, he still nurtures his disappointment at Jesus' lack of appreciation of him.

Only now Peter is seeing an entirely different Jesus, a Jesus whom he had never seen before. No longer is this the Jesus who walked on water and controlled the winds and rains. No longer the Jesus who magisterially preached to the thousands and dominated the minds of his enemies. No longer was it the Jesus who exercised incredible, miraculous powers to the astonishment of all.

Now, on the contrary, Peter is seeing a Jesus who has been overcome by these same enemies. Peter is seeing a bound, beaten, helpless, impotent, ineffective Jesus. For the first time, Peter experiences the stirrings of doubt and fear.

Later that evening in the courtyard where the torturing of Jesus continued, Peter is singled out by a maidservant as one of Jesus' followers. Fear then overwhelms the vestiges of faith and courage in Peter. He flatly denies having anything to do with him. A second person makes the same accusation, with the same denial coming from Peter. Early in the morning for the third time he is accused of being a companion of Jesus. Now in a terrified state Peter with an oath calls upon God to witness the truth of his statement that he knows nothing whatsoever about that man.

This third denial takes place at the first light of dawn, as the cock crowed in the distance. Jesus looks at Peter and Peter looks into Jesus' eyes. Peter then flees from the courtyard weeping bitter tears.

Were they tears that flowed from his love of Jesus? No! If they had come from such love, he would have returned to the courtyard and acknowledged to all that he was indeed the companion of Jesus. Rather they were tears that flowed from a totally new vision that Peter had of himself, the real Peter, the true Peter, the Peter he was when Christ was no longer alive in him. He found within himself the Peter whose fear and self love had killed the most precious part of himself as effectively as the soldiers killed the Christ outside of him.

For three days Peter, stripped of illusion, communed with this new revelation of himself. The bitter tears continued to flow as he experienced the real Peter within, this stranger, this frightened, disloyal, self centered, paralyzed, arrogant foolish person whom he had never met before.

The resurrected, fully reconstituted Christ appeared to Peter after those three days. Peter then experienced, welling up within him, a surge of joy, love, renewed faith, awe, enthusiasm and hope that transformed him. This time Peter was a purified person, humbled, free of any inflated self illusions.

THE COMING OF THE HOLY SPIRIT

This new Peter, unlike the old, knew that what he was experiencing within was not himself but Christ. This newly enlightened Peter could finally say with Saint Paul, "It is no longer I who live, but Christ who lives in me."[5] It was thus that Peter entered the third stage of his journey to God. For the first time he could see clearly Christ within, the mirror of the divine.

During the forty days following the resurrection Christ appeared many times to his disciples. One of these joy filled appearances took place along the shore of the sea of Galilee.

The Apostles were out on the sea fishing when they saw a solitary figure standing on the shore. John, the beloved disciple, recognized that it was the Christ. The disciples began to row ashore rapidly. Peter could not wait for the boat to land. He jumped into the water and rushed to the side of Jesus.

When the others arrived with nets bursting with fish, they found that Jesus had a fire lit on which there was a skillet with fish in it. In an extraordinary scene, they found the resurrected Jesus preparing a meal for them so that he might do what he enjoyed doing most, breaking bread in fellowship with those whom he loved.

It was in the context of this unusual meal that Christ turned to Peter and said to him, "Do you love me more than these?" Peter responded, "Lord; you know that I love you."[6] These words seem similar to those spoken by Peter at the Last Supper when he professed his love for Christ. However, they are entirely different words coming from a profoundly changed Peter. They now mean, "You know I love you because you, yourself, put this love back in me after I had killed it by my denial of you." Then Our Lord said to him, "Feed my lambs."[7]

A second and third time Christ placed the same question to Peter, receiving a similar response from him.

Each was followed by the same command, "Feed my lambs" and finally "Feed my sheep."[8]

Peter, having been emptied of his illusions about himself, is now filled with Christ and is prepared to bring Christ to others. If Christ had sent Peter out before he had reached this third stage of his journey to God, Peter would have gone out with the enthusiasm typical of his personality. However, he would have gone out bringing to others the illusions of Peter rather than the reality of Christ. The lambs and sheep of Christ would have gone hungry.

We have in Peter, then, a clear illustration of how one passes from the first and second stage of the journey to God, to the third stage in which they experience the mirror of Christ within. The coming of the Holy Spirit takes place normally only after a period of substantial growth of Christ within, a growth that can take place only after an equally substantive purgation of the many obstacles that hinder such growth.

The profound emptying of the flawed ego in us prepares for the birth of the mature Christ within. Jesus said "you will be sorrowful, but your sorrow will turn into joy. When a woman is in travail she has sorrow...but when she is delivered of the child, she no longer remembers the anguish..."[9] The entrance into the third stage is a 'birthing' process with all the labor pains that normally accompany such a process.

Jesus' statement that he must withdraw from his followers raises many questions. How could the presence of the human nature of Jesus existing outside them, become a barrier, an obstacle to the coming of the Holy Spirit? The answer lies in the dynamics of love.

Saint Thomas points out that humans tend to live in the senses. We are not angels, but embodied spirits. Part of the divine plan is that our first contact with reality takes place through the senses. What we see, hear, feel, taste and smell in the world outside us are the most evident and definite. We tend to be fascinated by the outer world. The world of inner consciousness is not the primary focus of our attention. Happiness is pursued primarily in that world of outer reality and not in the world within.

Divine providence adapts itself to this human condition. God's approach to us initially is through the senses. So, "The Word became flesh and dwelt among us..."[10] We can see this Word with our eyes, hear him with our ears, and touch him with our hands. He is alive to us in that outer world in which we find ourselves most at home.

Through the external presence and actions of Jesus outside, God begins to effect changes in our inner life. In the beginning the external, sensible, visible, reflections of God are indispensable to our ongoing spiritual development.

At a certain stage of development in the spiritual journey the growth of Christ within reaches a state of maturity. With spiritual maturation our spiritual development can survive without the external support system that brought it into being in the first place. When this stage has been reached, the continued presence of the external support system can become an obstacle to our growing awareness of the new life within us.

We are naturally drawn by our senses to the world outside. So, our fascination with the Christ outside can keep us from discovering the Christ within. In this way the Christ we experience outside can become an obstacle to this next stage of the journey.

This change in emphasis from the outer world to the inner world is always a painful one. Christ in the external world has brought us much consolation and life. Spiritual authors speak of the dark night of the senses when we lose sensible and emotional contact with the Christ outside.

Spiritual authors also speak of the dark night of the soul. This occurs when the inner support assisting us to experience the Christ within is withdrawn, forcing us to find his presence within in deeper and more subtle ways. That

93

pain, if patiently endured in union with the suffering of Christ, further intensifies the growth of the Christ within us. It becomes part of the condition of that growth.

Jesus said that it is only when the process of birthing is over and the woman sees the baby, that the travail of the birth is forgotten.[11] The awesome result of the birthing process brings the mother the joyful experience of the new life.

Jesus' withdrawal of his external presence from his followers was a prelude to his coming to full life within them at the first Pentecost. This withdrawal confirms a universal law of spiritual growth. Saint Thomas teaches that the perfection of love is not found in the external presence of the beloved, sweet as that may be.[12] No, the perfection of love is only achieved when the beloved comes to full life within the lover.

As long as we possess loved ones outside us, our love for them tends to remain imperfect. Their external presence excludes their intense presence in our heads, hearts, emotions, memories and imagination. It is only when the beloved is no longer present to us outside, that he or she can come to fullness of presence within us.

As a priest I am sometimes asked, when do I see the most intense love in others. The answer is clear. Love is in its most intense, deepest and least selfish form at funeral Masses. Without the external, living presence of the deceased in the coffin the mourners experience for the first time how radically impoverished their life has become. They become aware for the first time of what that person's presence has meant to them.

When God asks us to surrender to him the life of one we love, he is not quashing in us our love for that person. After all, this is a love he created in us in the first place. On the contrary, he is bringing that love to an entirely new level of intensity and unselfishness. It is God's way of bringing our love for that person to the relative level of perfection we imperfect lovers are capable of. He is bringing those we love alive in us in ways that they were never alive before, in ways that they never would come alive within us as long as we have their external presence.

This law is true of our relationship with Christ. A classic narrative of how many undergo their journey to God through Christ goes like this. They start life growing up in a loving Catholic family. They respond to devout parents and family members. They live in a warm, loving Catholic community, with priests and religious and apostolic lay persons who radiate Christ's presence to them. They can see Christ, hear him and touch him in their family and community.

In the family environment, they find it is easy to believe in Christ and his message. They find it easy to live in harmony with the moral demands of Christ's message. Indeed their faith seems to be strong. But it is a faith like Peter's, which is ten percent within and ninety percent sustained by their experience of Christ's external presence in others outside them.

Then they leave the loving family and go off to the secular world of business or the university. Their new outer reality provides a very different experience of life. They find little of Christ in their surroundings. They find a world much in opposition to what He stands for.

Suddenly they find that they no longer believe. They no longer care. Their religious values have no relevance to what this new world has brought alive in them. Like the prodigal son, they begin to live out the seductive promises of the secular world and to eat its forbidden fruit.[13]

Years later they find the happiness they bartered for has not been provided by their new world. They feel stirrings of hunger for the peace of soul they once knew. Like the prodigal son eating the food of the animals in his charge, they remember 'even the servants in their father's house live better than they do'. The stage has been set for their return to their true home.

Christ comes alive in them once more. He brings them back to that journey to the Father and the Father's house. Separation from Christ, experiencing life without him, often prepares one for his rebirth within.

Saint Thomas distinguishes the carnal man from the spiritual man.[14] The carnal man relates primarily to the outer world that he sees, feels and hears. For him it is the only reality. The majority of us probably belong to this category. Then, there is the spiritual man. For him it is his inner world that has primacy.

Saint Thomas sees divine providence dealing gently with both kinds. He finds a beautiful example of this in the different ways in which God led the shepherds, the wise men and Simeon to the discovery of Christ.[15]

Saint Thomas argues that the shepherds and Magi were carnal men for whom reality was primarily the world of the senses. Therefore, it was fitting that God would lead them to the discovery of Christ through external, sensible signs. Since the shepherds were Semites, and God traditionally spoke to Semites through angelic messengers, he chose the external apparition of angels to bring them the good news and to lead them to Christ. On the other hand, Saint Thomas points out, the wise men were gentiles and, typically of gentiles, were sincerely searching for ultimate answers in the stars. God, therefore, led them by the external guidance of a star to Christ.

Unlike the shepherds and the Magi, Simeon was a man of the spirit. He lived his life of constant prayer in the temple. Simeon located reality primarily in the world within. There his contact with God took place daily. Simeon, as a man of the spirit, did not need an external sign to recognize the presence of Christ. Saint Luke tells us that when he saw the young Jewish woman, infant in arms enter the temple, he knew immediately. Moved by the Spirit, he recognized the promised Messiah.[16]

Persons who are truly spiritual depend less on external signs. Those who have reached the third stage of the journey to God are more open to the movements of the spirit within. These inner movements of the spirit are not independent of, nor in opposition to, the external mirrors of nature and Christ in his Mystical Body. Rather, they are complementary to the external mirrors. All three work together to move persons forward on the journey to union with God.

Who are the persons in our midst who have reached this third stage of the journey? Who are they who are moved primarily by Christ within? We know who they are. Although we may not think of them in the terms I have been using. What are some of the characteristics by which we can identify such persons? Among their characteristics I would include the following:

• they seek more to give than to receive;

• they are interested in what they can do for the Church rather than what the Church can do for them;

• they are never lonely because they are never alone;

• they manifest a deep faith in the Church as a profound, living mystery;

• they participate in everyone's joy and sorrow;

• they are quick to acknowledge their many human weaknesses and may even laugh at them;

• they are forgiving and do not hold grudges;

• they spend substantive time in prayer;

• as Christ is the center of their life within, the Eucharist is the center of their outer world;

• they have little fear of the future and see in death the welcome embrace of God's love;

• they are always encouraging others to become more involved in the life of the Church;

• they seem to have little 'ego' and show no need or desire for praise, power, honor and other forms of recognition;

• they see all persons as children of God made in His image and likeness;

• they are free of biases of any kind, racism, pride of caste, elitism;

• they are acutely sensitive to the failings of members of Christ's Mystical Body, they suffer on account of these failings, but they do not criticize the Church;

• they are eager to proclaim the good news of Christ and strive to give witness to it whenever possible;

• they do not conceal their faith, but publicly rejoice in it;

• they evidence special devotion to Mary and accept her invitation to share in her son's sufferings as a privilege.

In a word, they are the true charismatics. Like Mother Teresa they mirror Christ in their words and actions. Their lives remind us daily that Christ is still alive and with us in this world.

When Peter and the disciples reached the third stage of the journey to God they became conscious of the mirror of Christ within. They had still not reached the face to face encounter with God. Their experience of his presence continued to take place by way of 'reflections' of that presence.

THE COMING OF THE HOLY SPIRIT

What had to happen to them to remove the final barrier that kept them from that immediate encounter? Saint Paul tells us that the face to face encounter will not happen to anyone while he still exists in this world. We must, therefore, pass from this world into the next to attain that loving union with God. Death is the door to such a union.

---

[1] John 13:38

[2] Matt 26:33

[3] Matt 26:34

[4] Matt 26:35

[5] Gal 2:20

[6] John 21:15

[7] *ibid.*

[8] John 21:16-17.

[9] John 16:21

[10] John 1:14

[11] *Cf.* John 16:21

[12] Cf. Thomas Aquinas *Summa Contra Gentiles* Book 1 Chap. 91

[13] For the parable of the prodigal son *Cf.* Luke 15:11-20

[14] Saint Thomas refers in many places to the idea that carnal men must become spiritual men to approach God, e.g. in *Catena Aurea* Vol. 2 S13 "Jesus is to be understood as about to change His Disciples from being carnal or animal-minded into spiritual men. A carnal minded man whatever he shall hear concerning the nature of God will understand it in a bodily sense; as he cannot understand it as being other than body …he thinks of them (the things he hears) in the manner of those who are wont to hear proverbs: as not understanding them."

[15] Thomas Aquinas *Summa Theologiae* Third Part Q36

[16] *Cf.* Luke 2:25-35

CHAPTER ELEVEN

The Door

Spiritual growth and the inner stirrings of
natural man

§

The meaning of death

§

The celebration of our true relationship with
God

§

THE DOOR

With the coming of the Holy Spirit the followers of Christ found themselves moved substantially farther on the road of interior transformation. They had advanced on the journey to their face to face encounter with God. They now lived each day acutely aware of the reflections of God's presence mirrored in the whole of creation surrounding them. They were sensitive to the reflections of divine love that they daily experienced in others outside them. They saw the love of Christ that filled the hearts of their fellow Christians in Christ's Mystical Body.

However, their most intimate experience of God's presence came to them from within. Christ, the mirror of the divine, shone within them. They now consciously identified in the stirring of love, peace and joy in their hearts, the presence of Christ. They lived each day surrounded by these reflections of God's loving presence both in their outer world and in their inner world. But the end of their journey, the face to face vision of God, still lay in the future.

They experienced within also, the continued presence of the 'old man' in them born of Adam. As Saint Paul confesses, "For I do not do the good I want, but the evil I do not want is what I do."[1]

Those inner stirrings of the natural man were always present. The movements of self-love, pride, lusting of the flesh and the will to power continued. All these inner conditions reminded them that Christ within had not yet come to full growth. They understood that it would only be when they had been totally transformed within, when the 'old man' born of Adam had been completely purified by Christ's presence, that the journey would end. Then, and only then, would the face to face experience of the Father take place. With Saint Paul they recognized that this total transformation into Christ would not take place as long as they continued to exist in this world.

When, would this transformation reach completion? What further changes would have to take place in them? How would the final barrier that kept them from the direct experience of divine love be eliminated? When would the barrier to the experience that their whole being now cried out for be taken away? The answer from Christ was clear and simple. It radiated down from the cross. They would have to pass out of this world to come to the direct, pure experience of divine love. They would have to physically die. Physical death is the door to the face to face encounter with God.

What is the connection between physical death and the beatific vision? How can dying contribute to the mystical, affective union with God? Is there some kind of magic at work in physical death that effects this union with God? Is this the real meaning of the cross? If so, why did Jesus not teach his followers to commit suicide? Why not gain union with the Father through a graceful and ritualistic self destruction?

Our previous discussion gives an inkling of the answer to this question. We saw how Jesus teaches that God is love, perfect, pure, infinite love. We also learned that the requirement for experiencing love in others is to have love in one's own heart. Without such love, the individual remains blind, deaf and insensitive to the love in others and the lovableness of others.

Since God is perfect love, it requires perfect love in the heart to experience God. Anything less than perfect love constitutes a barrier to the experience of God. Given the truth of this, it follows that perfect love in the heart is the door to the face to face encounter with of God. Furthermore, it follows, that there must be an essential link between perfect love and physical death.

THE DOOR

Christ teaches us that love involves a giving, a surrender of the self to the beloved. Perfect love, therefore, requires a total, free, conscious, joyful surrender of self to the beloved. There is only one way in this world that humans can surrender totally. A voluntary embrace of physical death for the good of the beloved is the only means to such a total surrender. Jesus states this simply, "Greater love no man has than this, that a man lay down his life for his friends."[2]

By voluntarily dying for us on the cross Jesus exercised perfect love. His death on the cross is both the symbol and reality of perfect love. His voluntary surrender of life on the cross in obedience to his Father and for our benefit, expresses his perfect love for his Father and for us humans.

In the garden of Gethsemane Jesus prayed "If it be possible, let this cup pass from me."[3] The Father's response to the Son's request was the Father's way of saying, "Love me with perfect love, and love my children with the same perfect love." Jesus responded with, "Not as I will but as thou wilt."[4] In this way he said 'yes' to the Father and 'yes' to us.

Catholic faith sees the perfect love initiated by Christ on the cross as other than a momentary phenomenon. It sees that love as an unending, eternal act, transcending space and time. It affirms in the human love of Christ the presence of divine love. On the cross the Father's love entered into and possessed the human heart of Jesus. Jesus' heart was filled with a love that was more divine than human. The Father's love expanded in Jesus' heart and through it emerged into this world in a radically new way.

Our association with Christ's death on the cross and with the perfection of love exercised there, is the key that opens the door to God. Catholics understand the Mass as our association with Christ's death. It is more than a mere memorial of an event that took place on Calvary two thousand years ago and is now over and complete. Rather, it is that very same act of love that was initiated on the cross, and which continues in its effectiveness into eternity.

The Mass places us in the path of that uninterrupted, love which erupts out of the human heart of Christ on the cross. Christ's love is a living stream that continues to flow into this world, daily renewing the extraordinary intervention of divine love into our human condition.

Christ invited his Mother to be with him at the foot of the cross, uniting her sufferings with his. She shared with him the privilege of giving birth to a new presence of divine love in this world. So Christ, through the Sacrifice of the Mass, invites all his followers to join with him in keeping his Father's love alive in this world.[5]

It is through this cooperation with Christ on the cross that he nourishes his growing presence in his followers. It is in this way alone that one can advance toward that perfection of love necessary for the immediate experience of God. Jesus said "If any man would come after me, let him deny himself and take up his cross and follow me."[6]

Christ on the cross teaches us that sacrifice is the language of love. The measure of true love is the willingness to sacrifice for the beloved. God's willingness to allow his Son to take on our human nature and sacrifice that human nature on the cross, is the revelation of the unlimited love of God for man. Only a God of infinite love, makes sense of both the Incarnation, the Word made flesh, and the sacrifice of Calvary. To deny the possibility of the Incarnation and the crucifixion is to deny that God is omnipotent, and that God's love for humans is infinite.

The following example is a rather crude illustration of the statement that sacrifice is the language of love. It also illuminates the connection in this world between perfect love and physical death.

Let us assume that you have a friend whom you think you love dearly. As far as you can judge, this friend's happiness is genuinely important to you. You somewhat idealize this relationship by telling your friend sincerely that anything you have is his. You truly believe in your friendship. Is this perfect love? Perhaps! Perhaps not!

One day your friend comes to you in dire need. Unless he obtains quickly one thousand dollars he will suffer painful consequences. You know that he is, indeed, speaking the truth. Now you truly love your friend and want his happiness. On the other hand there is also a very real attachment in you to your thousand dollars. Which love is greater, the love for your friend or your love for your thousand dollars? A choice cannot be avoided. No idealization of your affection for your friend can stand this test of reality. Sacrifice is the language of love, the test of love, and the measure of love.

This was the painful lesson learned in the courtyard by Peter about his relation to Jesus. He had to choose between love of self and love of Jesus. Until faced with that choice, Peter was able to idealize his relation with Jesus, and unconsciously falsify its reality. At sunrise before the cock crowed Peter denied Jesus.

Let us suppose that in the example, the happiness of your friend is indeed more precious to you than your love for one thousand dollars. You do love your thousand dollars, but you love your friend more. So, you graciously give your friend the thousand dollars he badly needs. Inside, of course, you experience pain at the sacrifice. Outside, you may smile and pretend that you are delighted to be of help.

Have you expressed and proven perfect love for your friend? No, you have offered concrete evidence that, indeed, you do love him more than you love your thousand dollars.

A month later your friend returns with greater needs. His situation has worsened in spite of your help. Now he needs five thousand dollars or the consequences will be disastrous. Now, you love your friend and you want him to find happiness. But your love for five thousand dollars is five times more intense than your love for the one thousand dollars. Once again, crisis ensues. Only, this time you and your friend discover painfully that while you love him more than you love one thousand dollars, you do not love him as much as you love your five thousand dollars.

Again we learn that sacrifice is the language and measure of love. In our present human situation, it is the choices we concretely make between opposing loves that reveal and measure the intensity of our loves. To say to someone I love you, but I am not willing to sacrifice my pleasures and comforts for you, is to reveal that your so called love for that person is a sham.

In passing, it might be observed that persons with many friends are the ones wise enough to demand no more of their friendships than the relationships are able to bear. Persons with few friends are invariably those who demand more of their friendships than the relations will tolerate.

All of this means that when a person is prepared to surrender not merely five thousand dollars for a friend, but everything he has, including his very life, we are speaking of perfect love. So, we come back to words of Jesus, "Greater love no man has than this, that a man lay down his life for his friends."[7] Human nature is simply incapable of a greater act of love than that of sacrificing one's life for a loved one.

It takes such perfect love to experience directly the perfect love that is God. Until a person actually makes that sacrifice, it remains unclear whether or not his love is perfect. This is the meaning of the cross. This is the meaning of the death of Christ as the Way to union with God. Christ tells us, that there is no other way, there is no door other than perfect love. Such perfect love in humans is exercised in the voluntary surrender of one's life for a friend.

The joyful surrender of life involved in perfect love does not mean that such a surrender is without pain. On the contrary, the more one loves life, and therefore the more painful it is to surrender it, the greater is the expression of

108

love in this voluntary self sacrifice. No one loved his human life more than Jesus. It is for this reason that he suffered more from the sacrifice of his life than any human ever could.

In the garden of Gethsemane, Jesus sweated blood because of the Father's request. He begged the Father, as no man ever pleaded with God, to do it differently. "My Father, if it be possible, let this cup pass from me..."[8] The second part of his plea, unlike the first, however, had no condition attached. "Nevertheless not as I will, but as thou wilt."[9]

Jesus suffered intensely on every level of his being, physically, emotionally, intellectually and spiritually. However, on the deepest level he experienced profound peace and intense joy. This joy was present, not in spite of the pain, but coming out of the pain.

Jesus knew the source of the pain. It came from the infinite love of the Father embracing his finite human nature, forcing through the limitations of that human nature a new presence of divine love in the world. Again, we are reminded "The kingdom of heaven is like a woman giving birth to a child...."[10] The pain and joy experienced by Jesus on the cross was the pain of giving birth to God's new presence in the world. If pain is inevitable in giving birth to another human being, imagine the pain in giving birth to God.

Saint Thomas' analysis of the dynamics of love provides further insight into the connection between perfect love and physical death. He points out that love involves a conscious attraction to the beloved. Such an attraction requires knowledge acceptance and celebration of the beloved.[11]

I cannot love someone whom I do not know. For my love to be deep, my knowledge of the beloved must be deep and true. Otherwise, I love someone who exists only in my mind. But love requires more than knowledge. Knowledge may lead to love, but it also can lead to hatred.

To love, I must accept the beloved. I must want the beloved to be the person that he or she is.

Parental love wants even more. It wants the child to mature and become everything the child is able to become. Parental love involves radical acceptance.

Love involves more than acceptance. It involves celebration of the beloved. To say to someone and mean it, "I thank God each day that you are who you are," is to celebrate that person. I know of no more loving words.

Still, love entails more than knowledge, acceptance and celebration of the beloved. Love involves the surrender of one's self to the beloved. Such a surrender requires that we know who we are, accept who we are, and celebrate who we are.

Since love is a conscious surrender of oneself to the beloved, how can I give myself to anyone if I do not know who I am? How can I give myself if I am confused about the meaning of my existence? Furthermore, if I cannot accept myself, if I am filled with self hatred, how can I give myself to someone else? Our culture leaves many confused about the meaning of human existence, and filled with self hatred. It robs persons of the capacity to love.

The above elements are operative not only in our love of other humans, but they are equally controlling in our love of God. I cannot love God unless I know who he is. I certainly cannot love God unless I accept the reality that he, indeed, is God. I cannot love him unless I celebrate him. This is what we call adoration. To say to God, and mean it, "Thank God that you are God," is to adore.

Christ came to reveal to us Who the Father is, and to teach us to accept him and celebrate him. He also came to reveal to us who we are, that we are children of God, made in his image and likeness, and created by him to share fully in his divine life.

THE DOOR

In this teaching we collide with the connection between perfect love of God and physical death. To know, accept and celebrate God in perfect love, I must know, accept and celebrate myself as a creature, a being who is nothing apart from God. I must celebrate the truth that my life is a gift. That it comes from the Father. That it belongs to the Father. That he can ask it back from me anytime, anyplace, and under any circumstances that he chooses.

It is only in dying that I come to the naked truth about myself. I am nothing apart from God. It is in experiencing my mortality that I come face to face with myself as creature. It is only by accepting myself as a creature that I can accept God as my creator. Where I am closest to my nothingness, I find myself closest to God.

If I sweat blood, if I beg the Father to allow me to continue to exist, but say with Christ, "Not my will but your will", if I give my life back to God as freely as he gave it to me, then I will finally have accepted God in perfect love. In the next instant, having passed through the door, I will find myself lovingly contemplating God face to face. Or will I?

---

[1] Rom 7:19

[2] John 15:13

[3] Matt 26:39

[4] Matt 26:39

---

[5] *Cf.* CCC 2182 Together (the faithful) they testify to god's holiness and their hope of salvation. They strengthen one another under the guidance of the Holy spirit.

[6] Matt 16:24

[7] John 15:13

[8] Matt 26:39

[9] *ibid*

[10] *Cf.* John 16:21

[11] *Cf.* Thomas Aquinas *Summa Contra Gentiles* Book 1 Chap.91

CHAPTER TWELVE
The End of The Journey

Faced with death we reminisce about life

§

Death destroys our sensible contact with
others but not our higher functions like
memory and love

§

After death we will become more aware of
the Providence of God

§

There is a process of purification after death

§

THE END OF THE JOURNEY

You have just died. A moment ago your soul still animated your body. You could see, hear, touch and feel yourself being touched. Your heart continued to beat. You were still in living contact with the sensible, visible, audible world in which those whom you loved moved about. Then your heart stopped beating. Now your eyes are darkened. Your ears no longer respond to sounds. Your sense of touch is gone. Your contact with the sensible world around you is broken. Your body ceases to be organized and enlivened by your soul. You are dead.

You had known for six months that this would happen. You had learned from your doctor then about the inevitability of your body's death. When you first heard this fateful word, you went numb. This numbness lasted for a time and then turned into depression and fear.

Then you entered an aggressive stage in which you sought out possible remedies to address your illness. Throughout this time you consistently turned to God in prayer, asking Him to heal you. Finally you gave a reluctant acceptance to God's will. With this acceptance a tenuous peace came to you.

While you suffered from physical discomfort, your mind remained clear and alert throughout your terminal illness. This added both to your suffering and to certain consolations that accompanied the pain. Your wife, children and grandchildren became your primary concern. With laser like precision you began to focus on your entire life from the earliest stages to the present. You did this at first instinctively.

Later, this reliving of your past becomes a deliberate, conscious exercise. You had long been an admirer of the confessions of Saint Augustine[1] and he inspired this spiritual exercise in remembering.

In his middle thirties Augustine awoke to the fact that God's love was at the center of his life from the beginning. That love had been at work from the moment of his conception within the womb of his mother Monica. It had been the controlling factor in every stage of his development.

Augustine, however, had been blind, deaf and insensitive to his presence. To correct this failure, Augustine set out deliberately to examine his entire life. His confessions are a conscious dialogue with God's loving presence in every moment of his existence. This example of Augustine motivated you to dedicate the greater part of your remaining time on earth to a similar spiritual exercise of remembering and reliving.

Reflecting prayerfully and mindful of God's presence, you came to see that past more and more through God's eyes. It was as if you were living the past for the first time. Conscious that your life on earth would shortly end, you saw as never before that the precious goods you loved were gifts of God. Of course, you had previously affirmed this. Now, however, you actually experienced God's love as the source of every good that daily came into your life. The experience at times overwhelmed you.

Your wife, your children and your grandchildren become revelations of God's love for you with a degree of clarity that you had not previously experienced. The rose bush in the backyard, the singing of the birds dwelling there, the warmth of the sun light touching your body -- all became living miracles and revelations of divine love.

In examining your past, you recognized the classic three stages of growth in the awareness of God's love. From your earliest years you were graced with the sense of God's

116

love and power reflected in nature. The lilies of the field, the birds of the air and the miracle of little children awakened in you wonder at God's creation. This wonder expressed itself in your fascination with the spirituality of St. Francis of Assisi. He was the saint with whom you most identified.

The second stage in your spiritual growth emerged gradually out of the first. During the first years of your marriage you became more conscious of the presence of Christ in the world. The birth of your first child was a reminder of Christ's presence in others. At that time you found Christ's presence in new ways in your spouse, your children and in the other persons, lay and religious, whose spiritual qualities attracted you.

You always had the sense of Christ's presence in the Church, his Mystical Body. In the second stage of spiritual growth you achieved a heightened awareness of that presence. Your awareness became an explicit consciousness of the Church as Christ himself. From that time on, you became more involved in the prayer life and apostolic activities of the Church.

Attendance at daily Mass became more and more the central event of each day. Participation in the pro-life movement attracted both you and your wife. You learned that your word and example had influenced others to embrace Catholicism. You began to pray more frequently for vocations to the priesthood and religious life. You hoped that, perhaps, one of your children would experience the call of Christ to follow him.

As your spiritual life further developed, you experienced a growing awareness of Christ within you. The movements of your head, heart, emotions, imagination and memory were affected. Your spiritual director told you that you were growing into the third stage of the journey to God, the Pentecost stage.

117

You now found yourself acting more and more in a priestly mode, consciously speaking and acting as the instrument of Christ alive in you. Your growing desire was to allow Christ to use your words and actions. You desired that Christ would make you an instrument to give birth to his presence in your family, friends, fellow workers and even in the strangers you met with daily. From personal experience you understood what St. Paul meant when he said, "It is no longer I who live, but Christ who lives in me."[2]

These memories reflected the good moments of the past. However, in your exercise of remembering, you were even more sensitive to the spiritual negatives of that past.

What came back with new clarity were the many failings. These failings stemmed from your self-centeredness, your pride, your desire to control, your many vanities, your exaggerated attachments to the pleasures of life and to the seductive attraction of your material assets.

As you recalled the weaknesses that infused your past and which continued to permeate the present, you understood with clarity St. Paul's confession "For I do not do the good I want, but the evil I do not want is what I do."[3] As you contemplated these past and present failures, you began to discern how God was using your memory to teach you lessons that you would otherwise have never learned. In a word, you experienced God's love at work using even your failings as occasions of grace in your life. And you understood St. Paul when he proclaimed, "I will all the more gladly boast of my weaknesses, that the power of Christ may rest upon me."[4]

The classic distinction between mortal and venial sin took on new meaning.[5] The difference between loving someone more than any other and that of loving a person as fully as that person deserved to be loved, acquired a new relevance. In those final months of existence on earth you could honestly say that you were not conscious of any mortal sins on your soul that had not been forgiven. You could affirm, therefore, that to your knowledge you did indeed love

God more than any other person or good. However, you knew also that you were still far from loving God as fully as he deserved to be loved.

During those final days God gently forced you to relax your intense grasp on the precious goods of life that he had given to you. He invited you to celebrate them with 'open palms' as gifts from him. You began to experience his love in them as you had never quite experienced that love before. His love filled more and more the vacuum created by your 'letting go'. You ceased clinging to them as ends belonging by right to you, and started to savor them as means -- mirrors and revelations of his love.

You ceased trying to find in them a happiness that only he could bestow. You knew that he was not asking you to reject them. He was inviting you to love them in him and him in them. You found yourself falling in love with this life with a quality and intensity that you had not previously experienced. In other words you recognized that your love of life and your love of God were undergoing a profound purification. Love of God was moving out from the center of your life to possess every aspect of your being, past and present.

Your loving relationship with your wife served best to assist you in understanding the purification process that you were going through in your relationship to God. From the time you fell in love with her, she had always possessed the first place in your affections. This fidelity to her never wavered in spite of the many human weaknesses that expressed themselves as your love matured. Yet, while loving her more than any other human, you well knew that you still fell short after forty-five years of marriage of appreciating and loving her as fully as she deserved to be loved.

During your final days of anxious concern about her and the children in your looming absence, you were constantly surprised by the strength and calm she manifested in dealing with your crisis. You realized that after all those

119

years, you still tended to underestimate her faith and strength.

You understood why you had failed to see these qualities in her before. Your exaggerated confidence in your ability to control life had kept you from seeing in her the strength that had always been there. You had to experience your own helplessness and let go of your desire to control in order to experience qualities in her that were always present but to which you had been blind. So it was with other aspects of her life that previously had eluded you.

Through the fresh relationship with your wife you gained insight into your relationship with God. A new realization finally came to you. After all these years of living daily with your wife, you were still failing to recognize and experience her lovableness fully. If this were true of the relationship with your wife whom you saw daily, you were scarcely prepared to see and experience fully the infinite lovableness of God whom you could not see.

You remembered the wise words of your spiritual director that only love in one's heart equips a person to experience the lovableness of others. Since God is perfect love, only perfect love in one's heart will remove the scales that keep one from the face to face encounter with God.

You began to understand more clearly the certain need for further purification of the love in your heart before you could experience the pure, infinite love of God. This very thought was on your mind when your heart momentarily skipped a beat and then stopped altogether. Death took possession of your body.

Your body no longer is alive and functioning as the instrument of your soul. Your mind is vigorously active. Your affections are intensely alive and specific. Your memory with wonderful clarity presents your entire life experience before you to contemplate. You are intensely conscious of God's presence, lovingly controlling you.

THE END OF THE JOURNEY

Nothing has changed in those higher levels of your consciousness. Only, your body is no longer involved. The bodily senses cease to provide data to your mind. The sensible, feeling supports of physical pleasure and pain have disappeared. You can no longer see those you love, speak to them or hear them speaking to you. You do not enjoy the sensible feelings of pleasure that their presence had previously brought to you. It is as if you are the one who is still alive and all of them have died and departed from you.

Your mind is clear, your affections are stronger than ever and you have total recall of your life. You have a heightened awareness of God's presence holding you in being and inviting your love. You are equally conscious of the presence of Christ in your heart. Since this presence is as yet not perfect it does not allow you to see the full radiance of His objective presence in your life. You realize that a further purification of the Christ within must take place before you can see the transfigurating radiance of his love in your entire life. In this encounter you are experiencing the particular judgment.

Since you have no sensible contact with life you can take no decisions or actions that merit further spiritual growth. It now remains for you to invite God's love to make fully explicit to you the radiance of its working in your life from the beginning. Your cooperation with that love now becomes more passive than active, though fully conscious and free.

Your present state reminds you of reading, while still alive on earth, about an American diplomat who had been kidnapped by an underground group in the Near East. He was held in solitary confinement for over five years. During confinement he was not physically abused. However, he was denied all contact with the outside world. He lingered in darkness without books, radio or conversation with other persons. He found himself all alone for months with only his memories and the affections in his heart for those he loved.

When released five years later, he emerged a profoundly changed person. Being a religious individual he was conscious of God's presence in his life. He was forced by a kind of self imposed violence to turn to God as he had never turned to Him before.

Upon his release he described how that experience had impelled him to examine his entire life through God's eyes. In turn, God became his sole consolation. The effect of this was a profound purification of his love for his wife, family, friends, the world and himself. He expressed no bitterness about his painful ordeal. On the contrary, he felt nothing but gratitude toward God for having enlightened him. He was grateful that his relations to all whom he loved were elevated to a higher level.

Recalling this story you realized the experience you are going through is not very different from the one this diplomat experienced. You had always thought of Purgatory as a strange, exotic, alien place unlike any thing that you might have experienced while on earth. You now discover that Purgatory is all too familiar to you. You have been here before.

You recall the suffering you experienced with the death of your father. You met with similar pain later with the death of your mother. With their deaths, you lost physical, sensible contact with them. You could no longer see them, hear them, laugh with them, share a cup of coffee with them. The painful vacuum left in their departure lasted for a long time. Because you had always experienced them in their external presence to you, it was as if they had simply disappeared from your world of reality.

Then something emerged out of this painful emptiness. You began to experience your father and mother alive in you in an entirely new way. They were no longer outside, but inside, you. You became conscious of new ways in which they came alive in your memories of them. You recognized their presence influencing your thinking. For the first time you came to fully recognize in your heart how much their external presence had enriched your life and how indispensable they were to your happiness.

When they were no longer externally present to satisfy your self centered ego needs, you finally began to see them as they existed, in the full richness of their individuality. You began to fall in love with them in a radically new way. You saw them more and more for what they were, wonderful gifts of God, given to you to reveal his personal love for you. You came to the realization for the first time that they were not your parents by some happy accident. God had specifically chosen them for you. You recognized them as mirrors of God, reflecting his personal love for you. So, you began to love them in God, and to love God in them.

You recall the teaching of St. Thomas about love.[6] The perfection of love is attained only when the beloved exists so intensely within, that his or her external presence, sweet as it is, becomes secondary to their internal presence. From your experience of the purification of the love for your parents while still on earth, you made the connection with what was now happening to you in purgatory.

Your sensible separation from all whom you loved on earth was intended by God to set the stage for the same purification of your love for them that had been effected by him relating to your parents. God had not taken them away from you. He was preparing to return them to you in a far more wonderful way, just as he had returned your deceased parents to you while you were still on earth.

In recognition of this loving dynamic you welcome the suffering accompanying it. It is a small price for you to pay to finally arrive at the deepest possible love of those you left behind -- loving them in God, and loving God in them. You recognize in this suffering the dark night of the senses about which St. John of the Cross had so perceptively written.[7] Your pain becomes a sweet pain.

123

By this time you know that there are only two ways of experiencing God's presence. The ideal way is to see God face to face. Not having this direct encounter, you recognize the second way. That way of seeing and experiencing God's love is in and through reflections of his presence seen in the goodness of his creation. Further, you realize that if you do not recognize the fullness of God's reflected presence in the whole of your life, you are far from prepared for the face to face encounter with God himself.

Purgatory purifies our love of all creatures to prepare for the immediate experience of God. It is a continuation of the very same process of purification that had taken place throughout your life on earth. Only now you recognize and welcome this loving process, while on earth you had difficulty seeing the process as meaningful.

You not only recognize God's love at work in your present suffering, you embrace it and actively cooperate with it. You know that the sooner your love for creatures has undergone this radical purification, the sooner you will come to that perfect, direct, intuitive experience of the infinite lovableness of God, and the sooner you will come to the perfect repossession of all whom you love.

As your love for these gifts of God is purified, the splendor of his reflected presence radiates more intensely from them. This intensified experience of God's love at work in the entirety of your life brings a new form of suffering. It reveals with painful clarity the mediocrity of your life. It discloses the small mindedness and selfishness that dominated your actions. It unveils the lack of compassion and generosity in your dealings with others. Finally it reveals the excesses in the pursuit of life's pleasures and the other failings that haunted your human existence and which still exercise a hold on you.

You experience a humbling pain such as St. Peter felt. When he once again found himself in the presence of the resurrected Lord he was painfully reminded of his denial of him. You feel utterly unworthy to be in God's presence.

Yet God's love keeps coming to you in spite of your sinfulness. You come to realize the experience of your defects is the necessary condition for you to fully concede that God's love is not earned but freely given.

You recall the powerful analogy by Saint Teresa of Avila between a human soul and a glass of water. Saint Teresa tells us to examine a glass of water in the ordinary light of day. It will appear to be pure and transparent. Then hold the glass of water up to the bright rays of the sun and you will see all kinds of impurities that went undetected in ordinary light. So also, when the soul becomes transparent in the direct light of divine love, its many impurities become clearly visible.

The pain of this purification comes from self awareness. You accept the pain as inseparable from the ongoing preparation for the direct encounter with God. In the experience of profound unworthiness you are going through, you recognize the dark night of the soul described by St. John of the Cross. So you do not despair. Rather your hope is intensified.

You recall listening to the music of Beethoven as a child. At first it had no effect on you. You experienced it as meaningless, chaotic noise. After several sessions bits and pieces of his music began to resonate in you. You came to recognize the connectedness between the seemingly unrelated parts.

In later years, after much listening, you were able to experience the genius of Beethoven in each and every note. You came alive to the power, beauty and coherency of his compositions. Each note related to every other note. There were no meaningless intervals or sounds involved. A splendid unity radiated from the multiplicity of sounds. The Beethoven incarnated in his music awakened the sleeping Beethoven dormant in you.

Something similar is now happening to you. You contemplate all of your life in the context of God's illuminating, loving presence. You begin to recognize in what at first seemed bits and pieces, the unifying working of divine love.

You recall the teaching of Jesus that your life is a masterpiece of divine art and love, "Not a sparrow falls to the ground", "The very hairs of your head are numbered."[8] You see more and more clearly through God's love the inter-relatedness of every part of your life -- the victories and failures, the virtues and vices, the shadows and highlights. The splendor of God's love shines through like a purifying fire that burns away the impurities of your ego and illusions.

As you continue to release your hold on the good things of life that you loved with too great an intensity, your loving interaction with God intensifies. You experience with ever growing clarity the radiance of his love in every aspect of your life. A kind of Transfiguration of your entire life takes place in which the infinite love of Christ shines through with greater and greater intensity. Like Peter, James and John on the mountain of the original Transfiguration, you prostrate yourself in the presence of Ultimate Mystery.

Saint Thomas tells us that love makes us identify with the beloved and that love seeks union with the beloved. Separation from the beloved or ill fortune on the part of the beloved produces pain. Saint Thomas points out God is perfect and he is always present to us. Therefore such suffering can never come from perfect love of God. From such love can only come peace and joy, which Saint Thomas identifies as the immediate fruits of the love of God.[9]

In Purgatory you know that God is perfect love and that you will in the end come to possess him and all you love. So, great joy and peace comes to you from this knowledge. At the same time you know that he is present to you and this adds to your peace and joy. In this sense Purgatory is a sublimely peaceful and joy filled state.

Yet, while God on His part is present to you, the impurities of the love in your heart still keep you from seeing Him face to face. While you long for this immediate vision, you know the separation does not come from him. So you beg him to continue the work of purification. You embrace the process wholeheartedly.

Oddly enough, the more you desire union with him, the greater is the pain of separation. You find yourself like a person returning home after years of separation from loved ones. The closer they get to home and to those they love, the more intense becomes the desire for reunion. Therefore, the more intense becomes the pain of separation.

God's love shines through to you more and more out of the whole of your life. You experience a release of pain as his love begins to possess every aspect of your existence. You are coming closer to the face to face encounter.

You finally reach that perfection of love that allows you to surrender every good back to him, Father, Mother, family, friends and your life itself. With this act of surrender everything in you cries out for union with God. Yet the face to face encounter still does not come. You cry out again, Now! Now! And it still does not take place. Then you realize that your will is still seeking to orchestrate this union with God. You realize you are still playing at being God. With this realization you turn to God and say to Him, whenever you will it. At that very instant you SEE.

---

[1] Cf. *The Confessions of Augustine* are an English translation of the works written by Augustine between 397 AD and 401 AD.

[2] Gal. 2:20

[3] Rom. 7:19

[4] 2 Cor. 12:9

[5] Cf. CCC 1855-1856 Mortal sin destroys charity in the heart of man by a grave violation of God's law; it turns man away from God, who is his

ultimate end and his beatitude, by preferring an inferior good to him. Venial sin allows charity to subsist, even though it offends and wounds it.

[6] Saint Thomas makes the point that our very ability to act depends on the internal operation of love since love is what moves the will. *Cf. Summa Contra Gentiles* Book IV Chap 19. He makes this point clear in regard to Christ's love by quoting Saint Paul in 2 Cor. 5:14 "the love of Christ controls us"

[7] Saint John of the Cross was born in 1542 and died in 1591. He founded the Discalced Carmelites. He combined the imagination of a mystic and a poet with the precision of a theologian and philosopher trained in the tradition of Thomas Aquinas. His poems deal with the purification of the soul in its mystical journey to God.

[8] *Cf.* Matt 10:29-30

[9] Thomas Aquinas *Summa Theologiae* First Part of the Second Part Q 70 A3

CHAPTER THIRTEEN
The Face to Face Encounter

What we know of the face to face encounter

§

The Good News

§

Heaven is like a wedding feast

§

The nature of knowledge

§

Embodied Creatures

§

The spiritual bodies of the resurrected

§

THE FACE TO FACE ENCOUNTER

What happens to a person who has achieved that perfect love of God that removes all barriers to the face to face encounter with him? What will their experience be? There are many questions about what the face to face, loving encounter with God entails!

These questions usually revolve around particular themes. How does heaven differ from earth? How does the existence of the blessed differ from their mode of being before death? Can the beatific vision be described.

Having never enjoyed this face to face encounter with God I am unable to provide answers to these questions from personal experience. Nor have I ever met another person who was gifted with this vision, and can answer such questions.

I have met persons, and some I take seriously, who have revealed to me that the Blessed Mother appeared to them. I have met others who claim to have seen one or other of the saints. More rare is the person claiming to have seen Jesus. However, I have yet to meet a person in this world who claimed that she had seen God, or that God had appeared to her.

I frequently meet persons who report having enjoyed intense experiences of the enveloping presence and embrace of divine love. Such experiences are quite common among spiritual persons. Everywhere I go in carrying out my priestly ministry, I meet persons who are truly holy, who live their lives in the presence of God and Christ. I am no longer surprised at my encounters with individuals who are saints, though they would be the last ones to think of themselves in such terms. I find them where ever I go. Again, I have yet to meet someone who claims to have seen God face to face.

Saint Thomas in his earlier writings, entertained the possibility that perhaps two persons while still in this world may have been gifted with brief face to face encounters with God. He considered this out of respect for the traditions of his time. The two men Thomas had in mind were Moses on Mt. Sinai, and Saint Paul on the road to Damascus. However, in his later years Saint Thomas backed away from this position for sophisticated reasons.[1]

Saint Paul in his epistles describes a man who may have experienced in this life the direct intuition of God. He writes, "And I know this man was caught up into Paradise -- whether in the body or out of the body I do not know, God knows -- and he heard things that can not be told, which man may not utter."[2] Some theologians argue that Paul is describing his personal experience, and that it involved the face to face encounter with God. Yet the same Paul says elsewhere, "For now we see in a mirror dimly, but then face to face. Now I know in part; then I shall understand fully."[3]

We read in The Old Testament in the book of Exodus, "Thus the Lord used to speak to Moses face to face, as a man speaks to his friend."[4] Moses, in describing his mystical experience on Mt. Sinai, tells of the burning bush and the voice of Yahweh speaking to him from the bush. However, we also read in Exodus, "You cannot see my [The Lord's] face; for man shall not see me and live."[5] Further The Lord arranges for Moses to see The Lord's back and again says "But my face shall not be seen."[6]

Jesus tells us that "No one knows the Son except the Father; and no one knows the Father except the Son and any one to whom the Son chooses to reveal him."[7] We read about Jesus taking Peter, James and John up the mountain with him. There he underwent a Transfiguration. For a moment the glory of his divinity shone through his humanity. His garments became as white as snow. Moses and Elijah appeared at each side of him. And the voice from heaven proclaimed, "This is my beloved Son... listen to him."[8]

Nowhere in the Gospels, though, do we read of Jesus bringing his followers to a face to face experience of the Father. When Philip asked Jesus at the Last Supper to "Show us the Father...", Jesus' response was, "he who has seen me has seen the Father."[9] But knowing Jesus in his human nature is to see there a reflection of the Father, not the face to face vision.

So we find ourselves on a journey, moving toward a goal that no one in this life has ever seen. Christ, however, does provide us with indirect insights into the mystery of the Godhead. These permit us to speculate about the beatific vision and identify some of the elements it will entail.

One of the teachings of Christ is that the whole of reality is a loving work of divine art.[10] Creation involves the embodiment of divine wisdom, love, beauty, power and riches of being proper to God. Therefore we see the reflections of God's radiant presence in the mirrors of nature, the Mystical Body outside us and, perhaps, even reflections of the divine coming from within.

Building on this teaching of Jesus we can offer the following argument. If one could reach out, embrace, taste, possess and experience the entire of the vast created universe, and exhaust in this embrace whatever joy and fulfillment the universe can offer, one would still be experiencing only a finite embodiment of the infinite riches, goodness, beauty and wisdom present in God. Christ says "What does it profit a man to gain the whole world and forfeit his life."[11]

The joy present in a minimal degree of direct, intuitive encounter with the divine reality would immeasurably transcend the joy potential in the possession of the entire world. This is true since God infinitely transcends the cumulative perfection of his creation.

133

This thought might be stated in a slightly different way. If one were to distill from the hearts of every human who ever existed whatever joy they have derived from the vast variety of good things with which God has populated the world, and this distillation of the joy of millions were to be concentrated in the heart of one person, that joy would still be one derived from the experience of the finite goods of God's creative work. The minimum, direct encounter of the lowest saint in heaven with the unlimited riches of God would produce a joy that infinitely transcends the cumulative potential joy present in the universe.

Christ, therefore, teaches us that whatever joy we experience in this life from any of the Father's creative gifts, is a foretaste of the joys that will be experienced in heaven. As one author states it, the joys of this world are like hors d'oeuvres preparing our appetites for the banquet planned for us in heaven. In fact, a good part of Jesus' apostolic mission was directed to assisting his followers to enjoy more fully the good things of this life precisely as preparations for the joys to come in heaven.

Jesus was severely criticized for this by his enemies. They accused him of being a drunkard and glutton.[12] His response was revealing of the promise of the life to come. "Can the wedding guests mourn as long as the bridegroom is with them? "The days will come, when the bridegroom is taken away from them, and then they will fast."[13]

Christ sees himself as a groom in his relation to his followers who are his bride. He compares his presence with this bride to a wedding feast.

For the Jews of his time, the peak experience of life was the wedding celebration that could last several days. It was then that friends gathered to rejoice in their experience of the loving presence of Yahweh and in their love for one another. When Christ was asked explicitly what heaven would be like, he compared it to a wedding feast.[14]

THE FACE TO FACE ENCOUNTER

There is a significant difference between the Christian Faith and that of Jewish and Islamic believers in their perception of God. All three major religious faiths are monotheistic.[15] However, Christian Faith affirms that within the unity of the Godhead there exists a Trinity of Persons, Father, Son (Word) and Holy Spirit. The mystery of the Godhead involves a community of divine persons existing within the unity of the divine nature. Hence, the encounter with God involves entering into a loving community of divine persons.

The wedding feast in Jesus' description of heaven involves more than a human, communal gathering, lovingly observed by God from without. Rather, it is a direct involvement in the dynamic loving relations that bind Father, Son and Holy Spirit. The divine wedding party has been going on from all eternity. Christ invites us to enter as guests. Christ teaches his followers on earth to see in the joy of the wedding gatherings in this world, a mirror of the joy eternally present in the loving relations of the three divine persons.

It is necessary to understand the nature of knowledge when reflecting on the face to face encounter with God, the Beatific Vision. Saint Thomas distinguishes two basic forms of knowledge. The first he calls speculative knowledge, and the second, affective knowledge.[16]

Speculative knowledge provides the intellect with the truth of a reality. It is knowledge we might say through the 'head'. Affective knowledge puts the 'heart' into contact with the goodness or loveableness of a reality through actual experience of the affects of the object. Affective knowledge, therefore, is practical, existential, experiential knowledge. It is knowledge through love.

We tend to think of the encounter with God more in terms of the affective than the speculative. God invites us to "Taste and see the goodness of the Lord."[17]

THE JOURNEY TO GOD

The face to face encounter surely entails both speculative and affective knowledge. In that Beatific Vision we know both the truth of God and we experience the infinite loveableness of God. The Beatific Vision entails, therefore, an immediate, practical, intuitive, loving possession of the infinite goodness of God. We will be possessed by God both in the heart and in the head.

This loving union with God involves more than a passive sitting and staring at the Godhead. It is more a loving embrace in which God draws us into an intense participation in the divine life. Christ promises in the Eucharist, "He who eats my flesh and drinks my blood abides in me, and I in him.[18] As the Father and I share the same life, so you will share this life with us."[19]

The life we are invited to share is the source of all existing beings. It holds all things in existence. Our participation in this divine life immediately places us into a new relation with the entirety of God's creation.

Consider again someone visiting the Sistine Chapel who is contemplating Michelangelo's masterpiece. Imagine that a stranger comes to his side and begins to point out aesthetic aspects of the frescoes that he had failed to see. As he listens to this person and begins to see the masterpiece through the stranger's eyes, it is as if he were seeing this work for the first time. He can only marvel at the new levels of his experience of the paintings when seen under the direction of the stranger. The stranger then leaves, and the visitor turns to the person next to him to ask, "Who was that man?" The person replies, "Didn't you recognize him? That was Michelangelo."

Compare the situation in the Sistine Chapel to what happened when the disciples heard Jesus speak about the wonders of nature. It was through the Word "All things were made."[20] The followers of Christ were seeing these wonders through the eyes of the very artist who created them. So, they saw nature as they had never seen it before. They saw nature as a mirror of the divine.

THE FACE TO FACE ENCOUNTER

Let us take this example one step further. Imagine what your experience would be if you could enter inside the head and heart of Michelangelo. Imagine that you see his works as he himself sees them. Consider the differences between your experience of the Sistine Chapel and the experience Michelangelo enjoyed when he contemplated the same paintings. Imagine, if you can, the experience you would have if you could stare out from Michelangelo at his Pieta, or Moses, or David, and see and experience them in the same way that the artist did.

In the Beatific Vision we will enter into the mind and heart of God. We will see and experience his creative work as he himself sees and experiences it from within. Imagine seeing the lilies of the field and the birds of the air as God sees these things that originated within himself and are held in being by his love.

Think of seeing your parents, family members and friends as God sees them and loves them. Imagine seeing the human nature of Christ and that of his Mother, Queen of the Heavens, as God the Father sees and loves them.

All of this enters into the eternal wedding feast. The feast, which with the communion of saints, Christ invites us to enjoy as his guests.

The symbol of the eternal wedding feast in heaven brings with it the connotations of food. By implication we are brought to consider the role that our bodies will play in that heaven.

At the heart of the Catholic Faith is the understanding that humans are embodied spirits and are not angels. We are not pure spirits experiencing an unfortunate, negative linkage with the material world through our bodies.

A number of ancient philosophies, including Manichaeism and Platonism, held the view that our souls, or spirits, were temporarily imprisoned in our bodies.[21] This view had led to the denial of Christ's bodily resurrection by Corinthian Christians.

Some Christian sects to-day accept the view that we are spirits experiencing an unfortunate linkage to the material world. The Catholic Church affirms that we are embodied spirits. The human body is an essential part of the perfection of human nature. The Church holds that our link with the material world is a positive one and that the material world itself is a gift of God.

Christ comes to redeem our entire human nature, body and soul. Salvation involves the full reconstitution of our intact humanity. The resurrection of Christ's own human body three days after its death on the cross is the clearest revelation of this truth. In the reality of the resurrected body of Christ we have our best insight into the reconstitution of our bodies in heaven.

What happened on that first Easter evening when the resurrected Christ appeared to his disciples? They were cowering behind locked doors in the upper room. Did they jump up with joy to welcome him? Rather, they cringed before him in fear, convinced that they were seeing a ghost. Christ said to them, "See my hands and feet, that it is I myself; handle me and see; for a spirit has not flesh and bones as you see that I have."[22]

They still could not believe that it was really him. He then asked them to give him something to eat. It was only as he ate the food they gave him, the most elementary of physical, human activity, that they finally became convinced that it was truly him, fully alive, body and spirit.

Later, when they reported the good news to the Apostle Thomas, he refused to believe them. His response was, "Unless I see in his hands the print of the nails, and place my finger in the mark of the nails, and place my hand in his side, I will not believe."[23]

Jesus again appeared in their midst and said to the doubting Thomas, "Put your finger here, and see my hands; and put out your hand, and place it in my side; do not be faithless, but believing."[24] Thus Thomas knew that the risen

Christ not only possessed a true human body, but the same body that he surrendered on the cross.

Saint Paul speaks of Christ's resurrected body as a spiritual body, having different qualities from the body that died on the cross. Writing to the Corinthians, Paul speaking of the resurrected bodies of the elect says, "For this perishable nature must put on the imperishable, and this mortal nature must put on immortality."[25]

Christ's resurrected body is, as Saint Paul tells us, the "first fruits" of the salvation purchased on the cross. Paul tells us that at final judgment our bodies will be resurrected as imperishable spiritual bodies.[26]

Saint Thomas points out four properties of resurrected bodies.[27] These properties characterize the bodies of the risen Christ and of the elect who will be resurrected at the final judgment. These new characteristics are agility, impassibility, subtlety and clarity.

Agility means that the body is perfectly responsive to the will. It appears wherever the will chooses it to be. Impassability means that the body is no longer subject to sickness and corruption. Subtlety means the body is no longer limited by material reality. For example, Christ appeared behind the locked doors of the upper room on that first Easter. Clarity means the body will radiate the beauty of the soul. Christ's body radiated the beauty of the spiritual perfection of his human soul briefly on the mountain of the Transfiguration.

One further question invites our attention. How aged will our resurrected bodies be, following the reconstitution of our human nature? Saint Thomas takes this very human question seriously. He conjectures that our resurrected bodies will be, approximately thirty-three years of age.[28]

His reasoning behind this seemingly arbitrary conjecture is simple enough. According to the tradition of his time, Jesus would have been more or less thirty-three years of age when he was crucified. Saint Thomas argues that Jesus would not have wished to offer his life to the Father one minute before life was perfect in him, or one minute following its attainment of perfection. Therefore, if he was thirty-three when he died, this must be the ideal age. Behind this thinking is the conviction that the resurrected human body will exist at its most mature, perfect stage of physical development.

With this somewhat pious insight of Saint Thomas I will bring this reflection on the journey to the face to face encounter with God to a close.

As I write down these thoughts, my mind leaps ahead. I look to the time when I, in my reconstituted body, will see with my physical eyes the resurrected bodies of my mother, who died at eighty-two years of age, and my father who died at sixty-four. The thought of seeing them as a young, vigorous couple of thirty-three years of age, makes the future promising indeed.

I also look forward to seeing the human nature of Christ with my physical eyes, and hearing his human voice with my ears, and feeling his embrace with my body. I think of my incarnated encounter with Mary, his Mother, and with Saint Dominic, Saint Catherine, Saint Francis of Assisi and the other inspirations of my life.

I think of greeting Saint Thomas, and thanking him gratefully for the many, meaningful insights I have gained from him into the ultimate meaning of life. I look forward to greeting Mother Teresa as a vital, young woman of thirty-three who approaches me to encourage me "to do something beautiful for Jesus."

I think, in a special way, of the tiny infants I have baptized, and then buried before they grew beyond their infancy. I look forward to meeting them as fully mature, beautiful young adults. I rejoice in thinking of the surprise and joy that they will bring to their parents who last remember them as helpless babies.

THE FACE TO FACE ENCOUNTER

    I offer a final word of thanksgiving to God for the gift of my Catholic Faith. Through this gift of Faith I rejoice with Saint Paul in saying, "Death is swallowed up in victory. O death, where is thy victory? O death, where is thy sting?"[29]

---

[1] *Cf.* Thomas Aquinas *Summa Theologiae* First Part q 12 A11 and Second of the Second Part Q 175

[2] 2 Cor. 12:3

[3] 1 Cor. 13:12

[4] Exodus 33:11

[5] Exodus 33:20

[6] Exodus 33:23

[7] Matt 11:27

[8] Matt 17:5

[9] John 14:8

[10] *Cf.* Luke 12:24-28

[11] Mark 8:36 Other translations use, forfeit his "soul"

[12] Luke 7:34

[13] Matt. 9:15

[14] *Cf.* Matt 22 1-10

[15] All three of the major religious faiths, Christians, Jews, and Mohammedans agree that God (Yahweh, Allah) is one in nature

[16] *Cf.* Thomas Aquinas *De Veritate* Question 18 Article 6

[17] *Cf.* Ps 34

[18] John 6:57

[19] *Cf.* John 14:7

[20] John 1:3 "Through him all things were made...and without him was not anything made that was made"

[21] Manichaeism has been considered a Christian heresy and as a separate gnostic religion. It is named after Mani a Persian who lived in the 3rd Cent. As taught by Mani salvation required liberating the soul from the material darkness in which it is trapped. Elements of Manichaeism have surfaced in later periods - notably in 12th Cent. France. Platonism can refer to many elements of the thought of great Greek philosopher who lived in the 5th Cent. BC. Plato's influence has had a continuing vitality to the present day.

[22] Luke 34:39

---

[23] John 20:25

[24] John 20:27

[25] 1 Cor. 15:53

[26] *Cf.* 1 Cor. 15:51.

[27] Thomas Aquinas *Summa Theoligiae* Supp. Third Part Q82, Q83 ,Q84, Q85

[28] *Cf.* Thomas Aquinas *Summa Contra Gentiles* Book Four, Chap. 88 [5]

[29] 1 Cor. 15:54-56

OTHER TITLES AVAILABLE FROM
SOLAS *Press*

Distributor Baker & Taylor Tele. 908 541 7508 Fax 908 704 9315

People from the Dawn: Religion, Homeland, and Privacy in Australian Aboriginal Culture

By W. E. H. Stanner and John Hilary Martin

ISBN 1-893426-98-X   Publication Date: October 2001

Paperback   168 pages   Price $24.95

The human equality of aboriginal populations was established in the 1500's when the Conquistadores were the dominant force in America. However, centuries later, the full personhood of the indigenous Australians was questioned. Here is an Australian work that shows the unexpected depth and sophistication of Australian Aboriginal culture

The Reality of Myth

By John Hilary Martin

ISBN 1-893426-99-8. Publication Date: September 2001

Paperback 138 pages Price $22.95

There is little appreciation of myth as a vital force. It is said that Westerners are deaf to myth and dumb in the presence of ritual. In this book Martin brings a new understanding. His scholarship is woven around the 'creation' myths in American Indian culture, the Bible and the 'Dreaming' of Australian aboriginies. Here is a seminal work that will open our eyes to the essential role of myth in culture and religion; its unsuspected role in science; and creativity.

The True Church: The Path which Led a Protestant Lawyer to the Catholic Church.

By Peter H. Burnett

ISBN 1-893426-74 –2 Publication Date October 2004

Casebound 768 pages $Price 37.95

Given pioneering California's stress on the practical arts it will come as a surprise that, its first Governor was a scholar. Peter Burnett was a magnificent pioneer of the "old west." Besides being a lawyer, soldier, newspaper editor, farmer, Supreme Court judge, businessman, politician, and statesman he was a scholar. In this book Burnett applies plain juristical logic to the question of the true church. His contemporary Orestes Brownson, said of Burnett's book, "Through him California has made a more glorious contribution to the Union than all the gold of her mines… In 2004 Cardinal Dulles says of this work, "Peter Burnett, applying the principles of Anglo-American law to Scripture and the Fathers of the Church, produced a remarkably full and impressive apologia…. Many issues treated in it are still lively topics of controversy."

This book is relevant today, as well as having profound historical value. The issues are indeed current –interpretation of Scripture, the role of reason in religious faith, the need for a tangible church, achieving certainty, and so on.

ORDER ON-LINE:

www.amazon.com or www.BarnesandNoble.com

ORDER DIRECTLY:

SOLAS Press, P.O. Box 4066, Antioch CA 90509 USA

Toll Free 1 888 407 SOLAS Tele 1 925 978 9781

Fax 1 925 978 2599 E-mail info@solaspress.com